7.50

Schocken

Berlin

69-19936 Nov. 3, 1970

BLACK AMERICA

SOURCEBOOKS IN NEGRO HISTORY

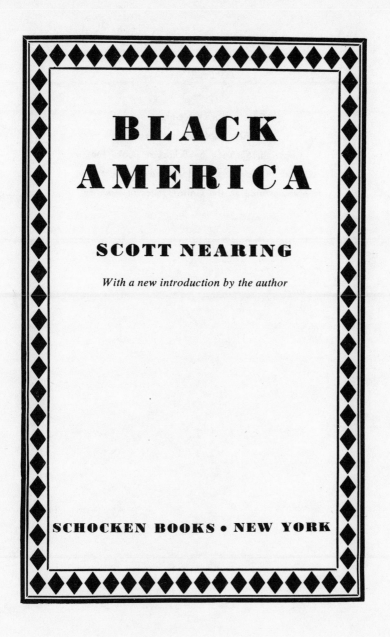

BLACK AMERICA

SCOTT NEARING

With a new introduction by the author

SCHOCKEN BOOKS • NEW YORK

First SCHOCKEN edition 1969
First published in 1929
Copyright © 1969 by Schocken Books Inc.
Library of Congress Catalog Card No. 69-17730
Manufactured in the United States of America

INTRODUCTION TO
THE 1969 EDITION

SINCE the original edition of *Black America* was written
and published in 1928–1929, the relations of Whites and
Blacks have changed in several important respects: (1)
inside the United States the Black population has increased numerically; (2) the geographical distribution of
Blacks has altered considerably; (3) Black penetration
into industry has increased markedly; (4) most important,
the Blacks have increasingly taken over from the Whites
the struggle for equal justice under law, the civil rights
struggle.

This struggle has also changed its character in three
directions. First, it has penetrated the South. Second, it
has become a struggle against discrimination and segregation. Third, it has become a struggle for Black Power.

While the Black proportion of the United States population from 1900 to 1960 has remained stationary at
around ten percent, the number of Blacks has more than
doubled, from nine million in 1900 to approximately
twenty million at the present time.

Sensational changes in the Black presence have occurred geographically. Blacks have moved from the South,
where they were formerly concentrated, largely as field
hands and domestic servants. They have gone into White
territory in the North, the Middle West, and the Southwest. At the same time, they have moved out of the
countryside into the cities; out of agriculture into industry and, lately, into commerce. They have also moved
out of unskilled manual work into the professions,
sciences, technologies, arts, and skilled services. For the
Blacks this constitutes a revolution of major proportions,
with the opening of a wide variety of possibilities and
new opportunities.

Organizations for human rights began after the Civil War. With the exception of religious institutions these organizations were built up with White support and, until recently, often under White leadership. Further, such movements attracted the Black professionals and intellectuals and made little appeal to the Black masses. Within a few years the leadership of such organizations has been taken over by Blacks. The civil rights struggle has involved White participation under increasingly Black leadership. Similarly, in recent years students and student-age Blacks have taken a prominent part in the struggle.

Black Power expresses the most recent phase of the unfolding Negro revolt: Black Power through propaganda, protests, and demonstrations; Black Power through the awakening of Black self-respect and pride in Black people; Black Power through the election of Black women and men to public office; Black Power directed to the unseating of the established order that profited by enslaving and exploiting Blacks and to the replacement of the White Establishment by a Black Establishment animated by revolutionary enthusiasm.

Internationally there has been a profound change in the relations between White people, on one side, and black, brown, yellow, and red people, on the other. Nationalism has increased. Racism has taken on large proportions. Generally speaking, before 1945 White people lived in the centers of empire—chiefly in Europe and North America. Colored people lived in the colonies and dependencies of empires—controlled, militarily occupied, and often colonized by the Whites. Whites were dominant in some colonies and dependencies, notably those of the British Empire. The colonies and dependencies of Japan were inhabited by Asians.

The conclusion of World War II saw four important international developments. First, the European empires were bankrupted and so downgraded economically that they could no longer hold on to their colonies. Second, dependencies, inspired by the self-determination formula, began asserting and winning their independence of imperial controls, establishing new Asian and African nations, and seeking membership in the United Nations. Third, the racialism upon which the central empires had laid so much emphasis began linking its racism to the nationalism of many new states. Fourth, a bloc of nations repudiated imperialism, turned to socialist construction, and proposed to replace imperialism and racism by socialist people's democracies. These international developments, symbolized by the outcome of the Cuban Revolution under Fidel Castro, gave meaning and content to the movement for Black Power in the United States. If the former subjects and victims of British, French, Dutch, and Portuguese imperialism in Asia and Africa could determine their future, why could not the twenty million Black people in the United States do likewise?

Colored populations in Asia and Africa have found it relatively easy to establish governments, mark out frontiers, and build nations and nationhood. They have problems like those associated with every drastic change. They make mistakes and try to correct them. But the problems and mistakes are directly related to each self-determining group, which has its own opportunity to count the costs and do better the next time.

Twenty million Black citizens are scattered among the 180 million White citizens of the United States, and they are concentrated in the southern Black Belt and in more or less segregated quarters of northern cities. They face the problems of segregation and discrimination, on the one hand, and of wide geographic dispersion, on the other, in a nation numbering about one Black man for every ten White, and with the Whites wielding an overwhelming monopoly of power and decision making.

Black America presented a problem in the 1920's and the 1930's. Arguments based on assumptions arising from race and color have been serious enough on a planet heretofore dominated and ruled by a White minority. Today matters are vastly complicated by domestic and international developments in a world in which the colored majority is presently demanding justice and taking the law into its own hands. Black-power demands from a ten-percent minority, in a nation predominantly White, present even graver problems.

However grave the problems associated with Black Power may be, they confront the American people, Black and White, and must be dealt with and solved by subsequent generations of Americans. Unsolved, they constitute a threat to the peace and happiness of America and of mankind.

SCOTT NEARING

INTRODUCTION TO
THE FIRST EDITION

"ALL MEN ARE BORN EQUAL"

AMONG modern empires none is more devoted to abstract principles of freedom and self-determination than the United States. "All men are born equal," declared the founders of the Republic on July 4, 1776; "Government of the people, by the people, for the people," promised Abraham Lincoln; American school children sing: "My country 'tis of thee, sweet land of liberty!" If declarations and professions could give liberty and self-determination, the United States would be a free country.

But the policy of empires is not made by moral precepts. Economic necessity is the compass by which the owners of land and productive tools steer the imperial ship of state.

Among the great modern empires only one contains a subject race within the homeland. The British Empire has subject races in Egypt and India; the Dutch Empire has a subject race in Java; the French, Belgian and Italian Empires have subject races in Africa; the Japanese Empire has a subject race in Korea. The American Empire, in addition to its subject races in the Philippines and in the Caribbean, has within its own national boundaries a subject race of more than twelve million American Negroes.

The matter is little discussed from this point of view, even in the United States. Almost nothing is known about it abroad. Yet the Negroes, who make up a tenth of the total population of the United States, have been, for more than three hundred years, the slaves, peons, vassals, servants, tenants and wage-workers of white American landlords and capitalists. Today they are the largest single American reserve of mass labor power.

The question has several practical aspects:

First—The Negroes themselves want equality of economic and cultural opportunity. Will this equality be "given" them by the United States ruling class?

Second—Filipinos and Porto Ricans are humbly asking the ruling class of the United States for "liberty" and "justice." What are their chances?

Third—United States economic interests are penetrating Latin America, and United States political and military authority is being established, with great rapidity, over the Caribbean. United States statesmen—Hughes and Coolidge at the Havana Conference of 1927-8, for example—assure the Latin American peoples that they have nothing to fear from benevolent Uncle Sam. Should the Latin Americans believe such statements?

Fourth—More than 150,000,000 exploited blacks in Africa and the Americas are striving to liberate themselves from the grip of the exploiting whites. Is the ruling white class in a democratic republic like the United States any more inclined to free the Negro than the ruling white class in a limited monarchy like Belgium or Great Britain?

The ruling class of the United States has come into intimate contact with two "different" peoples; the American Indians and the Negroes. Indian culture has been practically exterminated. The Indians that resisted the process are dead.

What can be said of the Negroes, who have been a part of the economic and social life of the United States for more than three centuries? Their experience should be interesting and instructive for Filipinos, Latin Americans, and any other "foreigners" who are placing their hopes on the much advertised sense of justice and fair play of the United States exploiting class.

This book describes the life and labor of *Black America* in the agricultural regions of the South and in the industrial districts of the North. The facts which it contains will startle no one who is familiar with the many recent discussions of "the American race problem." The arrangement of the facts differs, however, from that in the ordinary study of Negro life in America.

Black America deals with the American Negro, not as a "social problem" but as an oppressed race.

It proceeds on the assumption that no matter how industrious and law abiding the masses of Negroes may be, and no matter how talented may be the Negro leaders, the white exploiters of the United States will keep the Negroes in subjection as long as the Negroes are willing to stay there.

Those who are concerned with the course of modern imperial history would do well to examine the argument on which this book is based. If, as it assumes, the subjugation and exploitation of black men by white men is, at bottom, an economic phenomenon, the solution of the problem must be found in the field of economic reorganization. And if the struggle for emancipation must be waged by the black men themselves, the sooner they discover their logical allies and work out a scientific plan of campaign, the sooner they will win the emancipation they seek. Filipinos, Porto Ricans, Nicaraguans, Haitians, Cubans, Mexicans should study this book with great care. On its pages they will find a description of one of the precedents that the American ruling class will follow in dealing with other subject peoples.

American, European, Asiatic, African masses—white, yellow and black—who work and fight and pay for imperialism, might profitably think twice about *Black America*—as an instance of the temper of the United States owning class, and of American imperial policy toward those whose land and labor will yield a profit to the exploiting activity of white Americans.

Acknowledgments are due to the American Negro Labor Congress, the National Urban League, the *Crisis*, the National Association for the Advancement of Colored People and the *Labor Defender* and to many colored and white students of the Negro problem for pictures, data and suggestions. Also to Grace Maul, who typed the manuscript, read the proofs, made the index and arranged the photographs.

C O N T E N T S

CONTENTS

ILLUSTRATIONS

BLACK AMERICA

1: MAN STEALING

1: LABOR SHORTAGE

THROUGHOUT the English colonies in America, particularly in the South, there was a severe labor shortage. Land was free. The passage from Europe was long and hazardous. Men who had sufficient energy and initiative to cross the ocean were not willing to remain as wage workers when they could have farms or businesses of their own.

Tobacco, rice and cotton plantations were expanding in the South. Ship-building and lumbering were developing in the North. Both in the South and in the North there was more work than there were workers.

The American Indians could not be enslaved. They died before they would obey a task-master. They refused to work for wages. The colonists therefore turned to compulsory labor as a means of recruiting workers.

Non-free laborers who came to the American colonies were chiefly of three classes: criminals, indentured servants, and slaves.

The supply of criminals and of indentured servants was never adequate. Then, too, there was strong objection to the transportation of criminals, for many of them were rough, dangerous men. At a very early date the American colonists turned to another source of labor supply: the African Slave Coast.

2: BLACK SLAVES

THE first black slaves were brought into the American colonies in 1619. From that year until 1863 the African Slave Coast was the source of a regular supply of black labor that went into all of the American colonies and later into the southern plantation states where the large-scale growing of cotton, sugar, tobacco and rice made slavery profitable.

The Slave Coast was discovered by Portuguese navigators when they ventured down the western shores of Africa in search of a sea route to India and China. The profitable trade in slaves, gold and ivory which they developed led the traders of other European nations to begin a competition which eventually brought French, Dutch, German, Danish and English commercial interests into sharp conflict with the Portuguese.

Along the Slave Coast, which extended from Cape Verde, on the north, to Cape St. Martha on the south, lived various types of Negroes. Some of them were fierce and warlike. Others were docile. The latter were eagerly sought as slaves.

The natives of the Slave Coast had made notable cultural advances. They smelted metals, shaped pottery, wove, manufactured swords and spears of metal, built houses of stone, and produced artistic ornaments. They had developed a considerable and well organized trade with the interior. This native African culture of the seventeenth, eighteenth and early nineteenth centuries was confronted by the insatiable American demand for black slaves.

The slave trade began incidentally enough. The white traders were looking for spices, jewels, rare woods, gold, silver. They were not man-stealers. But as Negro servants became fashionable among the great folk of Europe, the slave trade grew profitable.

Ships sailing from the Slave Coast with a cargo for home ports made a practice of picking up such slaves as they could easily secure. By 1450 the number reaching Portugal each year was between 600 and 700. (Claridge, *History of the Gold Coast*, Vol. I. p. 39.) For this limited number of African Negroes the slave traders found a ready market.

When the whites first went to the Slave Coast there was little slavery among the African natives. Some captives taken in war; an occasional debtor, unable to meet his obligations; violators of religious rites, were held as slaves by the chief or head man of the tribe. At times such slaves were sold, but the slave trade was never established as a business until the white man organized it.

White men organized and subsidized the business of slave catching among the African natives. They provided the guns, the ammunition, the rum. They frequently formulated the plans and instigated the raids. The raids were made by Negroes—the stronger and fiercer among the African tribes.

3 : THE SLAVE TRADE

AFTER the prospective slaves had been captured, they were herded into stockades at the African shipping points to await the slave ships. Conditions in these stockades were shockingly bad.

Then came the slave ships.

Only a few hundred Negroes were carried in these early slave ships. While the voyages were relatively long, the Negroes were not sufficiently numerous to produce the horrors of later slave expeditions. The slave trade was still an incident of the general trade with Africa.

As the slave trade grew more profitable, larger ships were built, with galleries between the decks. Here the Negroes were forced to lie down, two and two, shackled together, with chains fastened to staples in the deck. Each Negro was allowed a space sixteen inches wide and five and a half feet long—where he spent the weeks or months of a voyage in a sailing ship. The galleries were made of rough lumber, loosely joined. Later, when the slave trade was outlawed, the Negroes were stowed away out of sight on loose shelves over the cargo. Where the space was two or more feet high they were stowed sitting up in rows, "one crowded onto the lap of another, and with legs on legs, like riders on a crowded toboggan." (Spears, *American Slave Trade*, p. 71.) Here the Negroes sat for the entire period of the voyage. During storms the sailors were compelled to put on the hatches and seal up the cess-pool. So atrocious were the conditions in these ships that the odor of a slave ship was often distinguishable at a distance of five miles. After four or five voyages slave ships were so filthy that they were abandoned. Negroes died on the voyage. Others went insane. Disease frequently attacked both slaves and crew. But with the fear of capture and condemnation for piracy on the one hand and the danger of a mutiny among the slaves on the other, the slave trader could do little to improve the position of his human freight. At best the slave trade was a hideous business. (Work, *A Bibliography of the Negroes*, pp. 256 ff.)

How many Negroes were carried away from Africa between 1450 and 1863? Estimates vary. Claridge states that the Guinea Coast as a whole supplied from 70,000 to 100,000 slaves per year during the early eighteenth century. (Claridge, *History of the Gold Coast*, Vol. I, p. 172.) Bogart estimates the number of slaves secured as 2,500 per year in 1700; 15,000 to 20,000 from 1713 to 1753; 47,000 carried by British ships alone in 1771; and in 1768 the slaves shipped from the African Coast numbered 97,000. (Bogart, *Economic History of the United States*, pp. 84-5.) During the years 1859-1860 eighty-five slave ships were fitted out in New York Harbor with a carrying capacity of from 30,000 to 60,000 slaves a year. (DuBois, *Suppression of the American Slave Trade*, pp. 178-9.) Other estimates vary widely. There is a general agreement, however, that during the years of greatest slave-trading prosperity at the close of the eighteenth and the beginning of the nineteenth century, the number of slaves leaving the Slave Coast must have been at least 100,000 a year.

Add to these numbers actually shipped from the Slave Coast, the Negroes who were killed in the raids, those who died in the Slave Coast camps, where mortality was very high, and the total gives some idea of the millions of blacks who were torn from their native villages in the course of three centuries to supply the American slave trade.

Why was the slave trade pushed so relentlessly? Because it paid enormous profits.

Some of the voyages went wrong, of course. But the whole trade netted immense returns. Along about 1800 a good ship, fitted to carry from 300 to 400 slaves, could be built for $35,000. Such a ship would make from $30,000 to $100,000 profit on a single voyage. Some of them made as many as five voyages before they became so foul that they could no longer be used. (Spears, *American Slave Trade*, pp. 84-5.) Spears writes: "No trade ever paid such large returns on the investment." (*Ibid.*, p. x.)

Britain passed the first law limiting the slave trade in 1788. The United States outlawed the trade in 1794. In 1824 Great Britain declared the slave trade piracy. These restrictions drove the trade out of Europe and centered it in the United States. After 1825 the slave trade was carried on chiefly by merchants from the Northern States. A writer in the *Continental Monthly* for January, 1862, stated: "The city of New York has been until of late the principal port of the world for this infamous commerce; although the cities of Boston and Portland are only second to her in distinction." (DuBois, *Suppression of the American Slave Trade*, p. 179.)

The slave trade was the business of the North as slavery was the business of the South. Both flourished until the Proclamation of Emancipation in 1863.

4: 4,500,000 NEGROES IN 1863

THE ancestors of the American Negroes were stolen in Africa and transported across the Atlantic chiefly in United States owned ships. Most of them went to Brazil, Cuba and the Southern States.

The census of 1860 reported about four and a half million Negroes in the United States. The number had increased rapidly. The slave trade brought in many new recruits from Africa. In the United States, stimulated reproduction added to the slave population.

The years immediately preceding the Civil War were years of considerable immigration from Northwest Europe. Consequently the white population of the United States increased more rapidly than the Negro population. Yet the increase of the Negro population was comparatively rapid—from 757,208 in 1790, to 4,441,830 in 1860.

In 1863, 3,853,467 of the Negroes were classed as black and 588,363 as mulatto (a mixture of Negro with white blood). When the slaves were freed by presidential proclamation in 1863 there were more than four and a half million Negroes in the United States. They made up almost exactly one-seventh of the total United States population.

Six-sevenths of the American Negroes were slaves in 1860. These slaves were concentrated as a matter of course at the point where slavery paid.

Neither Northern industry nor Northern agriculture lent themselves to slave labor. Northerners carried on the slave trade. They never employed slaves extensively, except as house servants, and by the beginning of the Civil War even these had been replaced by European immigrants.

Southern agriculture differed markedly from that of the North. The Northern general farm raised a variety of crops and was more or less self-sufficing. The Southern plantation specialized: in sugar, cotton, tobacco, rice. Some corn, pigs, chickens and other sources of food were raised incidentally, but Southern large-scale agriculture generally depended for its prosperity on the sale of one special crop.

Slaves performed the labor on these specialized southern plantations. Incidentally slaves did much of the building and other work of the South. A study of slave distribution at the outbreak of the Civil War shows 5 percent engaged in rice culture; 2 percent in hemp growing; 6 percent in sugar culture; 14 percent in tobacco culture and 73 percent in cotton culture. (Wesley, *Negro Labor in the United States*, p. 3.) These were the staple crops of the South and these were the crops on the production of which practically all Southern slave labor was employed.

Consequently a study of the geographic distribution of Southern cotton, tobacco, sugar and rice industries is, for all ordinary purposes, a study of the distribution of Negro slavery in the South.

In 1790 slaves were held in all states except Maine, Vermont, and Massachusetts. There were 3,707 slaves in Pennsylvania; 11,423 in New Jersey; 21,193 in New York. They were concentrated, of course, in the South: North Carolina, 100,783; Maryland and District of Columbia, 103,036; South Carolina, 107,094; Virginia, 292,627. Thus more than a third of the 697,624 slaves in the United States in 1790 were in one tobacco-growing State: Virginia. Georgia at this time had only 29,-264 slaves.

The cotton gin (invented in 1792) made slavery profitable over a much larger area. By 1860 slavery had been virtually eliminated in the North and West.

Of the 3,953,760 Negro slaves in the United States in that year, there were:

111,115	Slaves in	Arkansas
114,931	" "	Missouri
225,483	" "	Tennessee
275,179	" "	Kentucky
331,059	" "	North Carolina
331,726	" "	Louisiana
402,406	" "	South Carolina
435,080	" "	Alabama
436,631	" "	Mississippi
462,198	" "	Georgia
490,865	" "	Virginia

(*Negro Year Book*, 1925-6, pp. 225-6.)

Plantation culture of cotton, tobacco, sugar and rice were confined by climatic and soil conditions to Virginia, the Carolinas, Georgia, Florida, Alabama, Mississippi, Louisiana, Kentucky, Tennessee, Arkansas, Missouri and Texas. Automatically, therefore, these states became the slave states—the center of the American Negro population.

When the United States emerged from the Civil War in 1865, 14 percent of its population was Negro. These Negroes were either African born or else they were descendants of men and women who had been kidnapped in their African homes and transported across the Atlantic to help enrich the 347,725 American families which were reported as holding slaves in 1850.

The four million Negro slaves and the half million free Negroes who made up the Negro population of the United States in 1865 are the ancestors of the twelve million Negroes who constitute present-day Black America.

II: AN OPPRESSED RACE

5: THE BLACK BELT

THE overwhelming majority of American Negro slaves lived and worked in twelve Southern states where the culture of rice, sugar, tobacco and cotton made slave labor profitable.

The overwhelming majority of American Negroes still live in the same dozen states where their labor continues to enrich the owners of rice, tobacco, sugar and cotton land, as well as the local traders, bankers and other controlling white elements who dominate the economic life of the South.

The territory bounded by Pennsylvania, Ohio, Illinois, Indiana on the North, by the Mississippi River on the West, by the Gulf of Mexico on the South and by the Atlantic Ocean on the East is the center of the American Negro population. Within this territory there are considerable areas in which Negroes make up at least 40 percent of the inhabitants. This is frequently described as the "Black Belt." For all practical purposes, however, the entire South is a black belt. Throughout the South, Negroes make up about a quarter of the population. The South is the working place and living place of nine million Negroes.

The Negro population, as shown by the Census of 1920, was 10,400,000, or 10 percent of the total population of the United States. Since the present estimated total population of the country is about 120 millions, then, if the same percentage holds true, the present Negro population is approximately 12 million.

This is the census "count." It is a minimum.

Negroes whose skins are black cannot deny their race. But there are many Negroes whose skins are so fair that they pass for white. When the census taker asks his question concerning race, no white man can say he is black, but many light colored Negroes describe themselves as white. Where blackness is a liability, as it is in the United States, few men own up to black ancestry unless compelled to do so.

Geographically, the Negro population of the United States is very unequally distributed. In the whole of New England at the time of the last census there were only 79,000 Negroes out of a total population of 7,400,000. In the Mountain and Pacific States (the Far West), the Negro population was 78,000 in a total population of 8,900,000. The Middle Atlantic States, the East North Central States and the West North Central States (the heart of industrial United States) reported 1,393,000 Negroes in a total population of 56,250,000. But the South with a total population of 33,125,000, reported 8,900,000 Negroes.

Negroes make up less than 1 percent of the population of the Far West. In the industrial areas they constitute from 1 to 3 percent of the population. In the South, however, they are one-fourth of the total population.

The massing of Negroes in the South, more than half a century after the abolition of slavery, is one of the most significant indications of the restrictive power exercised by economic forces. Black slaves gained their livelihood on the rice, sugar, tobacco and cotton plantations before the Civil War. The vast majority of black Americans still obtain their livelihood today by raising the same crops in substantially the same territory.

Georgia alone, with its 1,206,365 Negroes out of a total population of 2,895,832, has more Negroes living within its borders than there are in the Middle Atlantic and East North Central States with their total population of 32,000,000. Incidentally, there are more Ne-

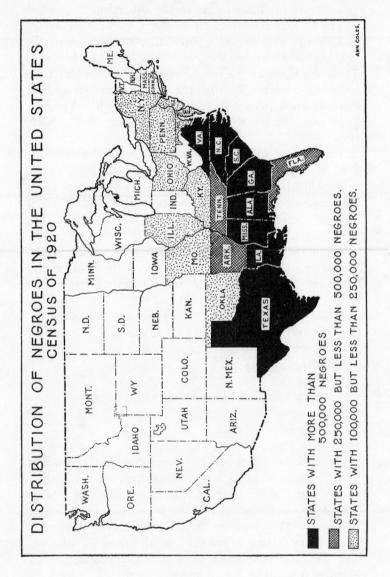

DISTRIBUTION OF NEGROES IN THE UNITED STATES
CENSUS OF 1920

ANN COLES.

STATES WITH MORE THAN 500,000 NEGROES

STATES WITH 250,000 BUT LESS THAN 500,000 NEGROES.

STATES WITH 100,000 BUT LESS THAN 250,000 NEGROES.

groes living in Georgia than in any other Southern state.

The Middle Atlantic States—New York, New Jersey and Pennsylvania—had a population at the time of the last census of 21,600,000, including 600,183 Negroes. These are three of the most important of the Northern industrial states. Two of the states, New Jersey and Pennsylvania, border directly on the South. Yet Negroes make up less than 3 percent of their total population.

The East North Central States—Ohio, Indiana, Illinois, Michigan and Wisconsin—had a population at the time of the last census of 21,000,000, including 514,554 Negroes. These states are the center of Mid-Western industry. Three of them border the South. Yet Negroes make up less than 3 percent of their population.

There are eight Southern States in each of which the Negro population exceeds the total of the Middle Atlantic States or of the East North Central States:

Georgia	1,206,365	Negroes
Mississippi	935,184	"
Alabama	900,652	"
South Carolina	864,719	"
Texas	741,694	"
North Carolina	763,407	"
Louisiana	700,257	"
Virginia	690,017	"

Proportionately, the Negro population in the South is vastly greater than in any other section of the United States. In the Northern Central and Western States, 1, 2, or at most 3 percent of the population in the state, is Negro. Ten Southern States have a Negro population of more than 25 percent of the total population. The six Southern States in which the proportion of Negroes is greatest are:

Mississippi	52.2	percent Negro
South Carolina	51.4	" "
Georgia	41.7	" "
Louisiana	38.9	" "
Alabama	38.4	" "
Florida	34.0	" "

Negroes make up 28.4 percent of the population in the East South Central States. These states include the Carolinas, Georgia, Florida, Alabama.

Negroes make up 20.1 percent of the population of the West South Central States. Included in these states are Mississippi, Louisiana and Texas.

Negroes are concentrated in the South. Even there, however, they are not equally distributed. Take Mississippi as an example. The population of the entire state is more than half Negro, but in Hawamba County, out of a total population of 15,647 only 1,074 are Negroes; in Neshoba County, population 19,303, Negroes, 2,949; Prentiss County, population 17,606, Negroes, 2,436; Smith County, population 16,178, Negroes, 2,594. These counties are overwhelmingly white. On the other hand: Adams County, population, 22,183, Negroes, 15,245; Coahoma County, population, 41,511, Negroes, 35,205; DeSoto County, population, 24,358, Negroes, 18,438; Humphreys County, population, 19,192, Negroes, 15,781; Jefferson County, population, 15,946, Negroes, 11,959. These counties are overwhelmingly Negro.

Other Southern states show similar irregularities in the distribution of the Negro population. At some points it is sparse, while other areas are almost entirely Negro.

This variation in the Negro population is largely due to economic causes. Negroes live in those portions of the South where cotton, rice, tobacco and sugar can be profitably raised. The Negro population is concentrated in these agricultural areas. Throughout the mountainous districts, where the Southern "poor whites" make up the bulk of the population, and where none of the staple Southern crops can be raised, Negroes are as rare as they are in rural New England. The distribution of Southern Negroes follows the line of economic opportunity drawn by soil fertility and climate.

The South has been rapidly industrializing itself since 1880. Its staple activities, however, are still agricultural, and the mass labor upon which Southern agriculture depends is the Negro.

Work on the land is the chief occupation of American Negroes. When the Census of 1920 was taken there were 41,614,248 gainfully occupied persons. Among them 10,953,158 were at work in agriculture.

Note the contrast with the Negro population: gainfully occupied Negroes, 4,824,151; Negroes engaged in agricultural occupations, 2,178,888.

A quarter of the population at large is engaged in agriculture. Among Negroes, however, the proportion of gainfully occupied persons engaged in agriculture is 45 percent.

Southern agriculture is a black man's country just as Northern industry is a white man's country. The agricultural labor over great sections of the South is performed by Negroes, as the industrial labor of the North is performed by whites.

The black worker of the South does not own his country. He does not even share with his Northern fellow-worker the illusion of "running" it. He merely lives in it, conforms to the social standards set by its white masters and performs its heaviest labor. Millions of toiling black exploited men and women and children have been the basis of Southern prosperity for more than one hundred years as they are the basis of Southern prosperity today.

6: LAND OWNERSHIP

NEGROES in the Black Belt do not own the land they cultivate. The great majority of them throughout the South are hired farm laborers or tenant farmers.

The total number of farmers in the United States at the time of the last Census was 6,448,000. Of these farmers 38.1 percent were tenants.

Six-sevenths of the farmers in the United States were white (5,498,000). Among the white farmers the percentage of tenants was 31.7.

The same Census reported 925,708 Negro farmers— less than one-sixth of the total. Among these Negro farmers three-fourths (76.2 percent) were tenants. Tenancy among Negro farmers was therefore two and a half times as great as tenancy among white farmers.

These figures summarize the general relation of white farmers to Negro farmers throughout the United States. The economic dependence of the Negroes is of course intensified in the South. While the Negroes form almost exactly one-tenth of the total population of the United States, they make up nearly one-sixth of the total number of farmers. At the same time they constitute almost one-half of the tenant farmers of the country. "In the South alone, where most of the colored farmers are found, the tenancy percentage of white farmers was 38.9 and for colored farmers 76.2 percent." (U. S. Census of 1920, Monograph 4, *Farm Tenancy in the United States*, p. 72.)

The United States Census Bureau issued a special Census of Agriculture in 1927. One volume of this Census, devoted to the South, contains a section on farm tenure in 1925.

Throughout the South in 1925 there were 2,299,963 white farmers and 831,455 Negro farmers. Negro farmers therefore made up about one-fourth of all Southern farmers. Incidentally, nine-tenths of all the Negro farmers in the United States were in the South.

Among the white farmers in the South almost exactly one-half (1,173,778) owned their farms in full. Less than one-fifth of the Negroes, however (159,651), reported full ownership of their farms.

The Agricultural Census shows 965,051 white tenant farmers in the South and 636,248 Negro tenant farmers in the South. Thus, while the Negro farms constitute only one-fourth of the total farms in the South, Negro tenant farms make up two-fifths of the total tenant farms in the South.

Tenant farming among Negroes is particularly prevalent in those states which have an unusually large Negro population. Georgia, for example, has 165,018 white farmers and 84,077 Negro farmers. The proportion of white farmers to Negro farmers is thus almost exactly two to one. More than two-fifths of the white farmers (71,076) own their farms in full. Among the Negro farmers the number of full farm owners is but 10,032, that is, less than one-eighth of the Negro farmers of the state. White tenant farms in Georgia number 86,802; Negro tenant farms, 72,206, a ratio of eight white tenant farms to seven Negro tenant farms.

Practically the same situation exists in Alabama where there are 152,310 white farmers, of whom 86,329 own their farms in full, and 85,321 Negro farmers of whom 10,953 own their farms in full. The number of white and Negro tenant farmers in Alabama is almost exactly the same (73,396 white and 70,539 Negro).

Both South Carolina and Mississippi report more colored farmers than white farmers. In South Carolina the figures are: white, 82,186; colored, 90,581; Mississippi: white, 107,086; Negro, 150,142. White farmers in South Carolina own their farms in full in nearly half the cases (37,925). Negro farmers, however, own their homes fully in less than one-sixth of the cases (14,476). The number of white tenants (40,251) is only a little more than half the number of Negro tenants (72,179).

Figures for Mississippi are similar save that the proportion of Negroes fully owning their farms is only one-ninth of the total and the number of Negro tenants (130,796) is three times the number of white tenants (44,946). (Census of Agriculture, 1925, Part II, "Southern States," p. 15.)

Evidently, then, even in agriculture, the field in which Negroes have been chiefly employed since they came to the United States as slaves, most of the Negroes are wage workers or tenant farmers. Only a small percentage of them are owning farmers.

With the passing of the years the proportion of tenants among the Negroes has increased. Census reports show the percentage of farm tenancy among Negroes:

74.6 percent in 1900
75.3 percent in 1910
76.3 percent in 1920

Between 1910 and 1920 the number of white tenant farmers increased 3.8 percent. During the same years the number of Negro tenant farmers increased 4.8 percent.

The United States Department of Agriculture (Bulletin 1404, April, 1926, pp. 7-8) gives the figures for Negro farm tenancy in Southampton County, Virginia. In 1880 the Negroes held 1,648 farms, of which 45 percent were farmed by tenants. By 1920 Negroes farmed more than double the number of farms: 3,550. However, 59.2 percent of them were tenants. Thus the proportion of tenancy among Negro farmers in this county had increased nearly one-third in 40 years.

During reconstruction days numerous experiments were made with different forms of Negro farming. Out of these experiments the system of share cropping gradually developed. Today it is the system under which most of the Negro tenant farmers work their land.

The share crop system is an arrangement by which the land owner supplies tools, machinery, seed and other necessary farm equipment. In return for these advances the farmer pays the landowner a stipulated share of the crop—ordinarily fifty percent.

Certain landlords, in addition to providing the capital equipment necessary to farm the land, make advances to the tenant in the form of food, clothing and other personal necessaries. The amount of these advances is deducted by the landowner from the share of the crop belonging to the tenant.

A very full description of various classes of Negro tenant farmers in the South will be found in T. J. Woofter's *Negro Migration*, Chapter IV, "Life of the Tenant Classes."

Under any one of these cropping arrangements the landlord keeps the books and usually sells the crop. As bookkeeper he may short-change the tenant. As crop salesman he may act as his own broker, buying the crop from the Negro at a low price and selling it on the market on his own account at a higher price.

Advances made by landlords either for capital equipment or for personal necessaries must be paid for by the tenants before the latter are permitted to leave the property of the landlord. Governor Hugh M. Dorsey of Georgia, in a public statement issued April 22, 1921, cites a number of cases where Negro workers in Georgia were held on the land against their will and when they left it for the city were arrested and sent back to the land. Here are some typical cases:

"A Negro worked for a farmer in County No. 7 for the last six or seven years. The contract called for a certain wage, but the employer would pay him what he chose. The Negro left three or four times, but was always brought back.

"The year 1920, he was to receive $25 a month and board. At Christmas, the Negro asked his employer how much the employer owed him. The man told him $65, and paid him $10. The Negro left and came to Atlanta where he was arrested and carried back, January 26, 1921."

"Another Negro was arrested in Atlanta and fined $25 for keeping late hours. The same white man paid the fine in April, 1920, and carried the Negro to the farm to work upon a promise of $40 per month, board and lodging. Three other Negroes were carried there at the same time. He remained for four months, when he escaped. He was caught and carried back, severely whipped and locked up.

"He was whipped twice. He claims to have seen another Negro beaten and then shot by a Negro for running away, and at the instance of the white." (Dorsey, *As to the Negro in Georgia*, pp. 6-7).

One Georgia planter killed 11 Negroes on his place, according to Governor Dorsey's report, in order to prevent them from revealing the conditions under which they were forced to labor. (Dorsey, *As to the Negro in Georgia*, p. 8.)

Negro tenant farmers find themselves little better off in many instances than they were in the days of slavery. They are attached to the land. If they leave it they are pursued or brought back and in many cases severely punished. Since the machinery of justice is exclusively in the hands of the whites, the Negro tenant farmer has extreme difficulty in getting his wrongs heard anywhere in the Black Belt.

If the position of the Negro tenant farmer is little better than that of the slave before the Civil War, the responsibility of the white Southern landowner is far less than that of the former slaveholder. On the eve of the Civil War, first class male slaves were worth as much as $1,800. A score of slaves thus represented a very considerable property, which any intelligent landowner was bound to conserve. The modern tenant farmer either represents no capital outlay, or else the comparatively small amounts which the landlord advances against his share of the crop.

Under such circumstances, why is it not possible for Negro farmers to become sufficiently prosperous so that they are no longer dependent upon the whites for advances? There are, of course, many Negro farmers who are in this class. The danger which they run, however, is considerable. If by thrift, industry or luck the Negro succeeds in joining the class of prosperous farmers, his white neighbors frequently take revenge upon him for the improvement which he has been able to make in his economic position.

Governor Dorsey's statement cites one such instance in great detail. The case is headed: "A Thrifty Negro."

The Negro farmer had saved, and bought a farm of 140 acres, where he lived with his wife and 12 children. Three of his daughters were school teachers. The farm was well stocked.

During the war, this Negro was so active in organizing the sale of Liberty Bonds and Thrift Stamps that he was praised in the local press. A white neighbor, when the laudatory article appeared in the newspaper, remarked that the Negro was getting "too damned prosperous and biggity for a nigger."

Trouble began.

The white man had his land surveyed; ran his line 25 feet over onto the Negro's property; drove stakes along this new line and warned the Negro not to trespass. The Negro disregarded the warning and plowed to his old line.

One Saturday afternoon the Negro with his three daughters and son went to town. The town marshal came up to him in the street and said, "I have a warrant for you." An altercation ensued. The marshal struck the Negro, knocking him to the ground. Several other white men rushed upon him and began to choke and beat him.

"Two of his daughters started to him. A man kicked one girl in the stomach. The other reached her father and began to wipe the blood from his face. The three were quickly overpowered. The third daughter and the son were caught. All were locked in jail. The girl who was kicked was menstruating. The blow made her deathly sick. She lay in jail moaning and begging that something be done for her, and for her father, who was bleeding badly from his wounds. The sheriff locked them in and left them without medical attention and ignorant of the charge against them.

"Next morning the Negro learned that his neighbor had sworn out a warrant against him for trespass. The sheriff refused to tell him what the charge was against his son and daughters. The Negro employed a lawyer. Then he found that he and his daughters were charged with resisting an officer in the discharge of his duty, his son with carrying a pistol. Only one witness claimed to have seen the pistol. This was the white neighbor who said that he had seen the son put the pistol in the buggy while the crowd was on his father. The buggy was searched. The pistol was not found.

"Talk of lynching the Negro and his family caused their removal to another county. . . .

"The man, his daughters and son were tried in the Superior Court. The father was sentenced to serve twelve months in the chain gang and pay a fine of $250. The girls were fined $50 each. The son was fined $100. The Negro paid the fines of his children.

"The man's smaller children and his wife were in his home while he was in jail. A mob, led by the town marshal, went to the house, kicked the door and demanded admittance, then shot up the house and went away. This was night.

"Next morning, the woman with her children fled from her home, never to return.

"A friend went by night and removed the live stock belonging to the family, and sold it for them at a great sacrifice. Their crop was a total loss. They will be lynched, it is said, if any of them ever return to their home.

"The education of his children and the success of his thrift seem to be the sole offense of the Negro." (Dorsey, *As to the Negro in Georgia*, pp. 17-18.)

Negro farmers are usually tenant farmers. In the comparatively small number of instances where they have succeeded in becoming farm owners, thus establishing membership in the ruling class, they are treated as outcasts and enemies and frequently punished for their temerity. The Negro who succeeds courts disaster.

1. Negro boy ploughing with a mule. Mules do most of the farm work in the Black Belt.

2. Negro girls cutting corn stalks with field hoes, Florence, S. C.

3. A young Alabama cotton picker.

4. Bringing the cotton in from the field and dumping it into hampers, near Oxford, Alabama.

5. Picked cotton, stacked, ready for weighing. Pickers are paid by the pound. Shreveport, La.

6. Two Negro children picking cotton near Florence, S. C. Small girl is six years old.

7. *Cattle still play a role in Southern farming. A one-cow plough, Alabama.*

8. *Ploughing and planting with oxen, Boligee, Alabama.*

9. *A hoe-crew of Negro men and women in a young cotton field, Aliceville, Alabama.*

10. *Negro women "chopping" with the long Southern field hoes, Marlboro, S. C.*

11. Negro boy and mule hilling tomatoes with a shovel plough.

12. Negro cabin, Florence, S. C. Neat and well kept. The whole door-yard was swept as far as the road.

14. *Negro cottage on James Island, near Charleston, S. C.*

13. *Negro girl carrying baby, James Island, Charleston, S. C.*

15. A Negro grocery store and dwelling house—typical of many of the Southern Negro business places, Florence, S. C.

16. A Negro cabin, Micro, N. C.

1. Row of Negro houses, Twenty-First and East Franklin Streets, Richmond, Va.

2. A "street" in Negro section of a Florida town— overgrown, rutted, almost impassable.

3. *Lilienthal Row, Charleston, S. C. A 40-room house, accommodating 40 families. There are 4 outside faucets and 4 outside toilets for the entire house.*

4. *Negro dwellings, Charleston, S. C.*

5. *The cotton comes to be ginned in town, Anniston, Alabama.*

6. *The cotton gin, Oxford, Alabama.*

7. Rag Pickers, Alabama.

8. Negro cottages and church, Hobson, Alabama.

9. *The cotton bales as they come from the gin, Alabama.*

10. *Waiting for bale. Negro woman with her mules, after the cotton has entered the gin. Alabama.*

11. *Waiting at the gin with his load of cotton, Anniston, Alabama.*

12. *The cotton mill from which Negroes are excluded by law. Alabama.*

13. Barber shop and shoe-shine parlor, Oxford, Alabama.

14. The wagon shop, Oxford, Alabama.

15. Negro children in front of Negro houses, Richmond, Va.

16. Negro with his mule. On their way back to the cabin, Florence, S. C.

7: WAGES AND INCOME

HUNDREDS of thousands of Southern Negroes work as croppers on land owned by Southern whites. Other hundreds of thousands are field hands: ploughing, hoeing, harvesting vegetables, picking cotton, cutting cane, for a daily or monthly wage. The Census Volume on Occupations (1920) reports 664,567 male Negroes and 527,937 female Negroes ten years of age or over occupied as farm laborers. The Census was taken January 1, when employment of farm labor was at a very low point. Among these Negro wage workers there are large numbers of women and children—some of the latter as young as six or seven years of age.

Negro tenants and Negro agricultural workers live upon the same general economic level, close to the margin of subsistence. Their shacks and cabins are much the same in character. Their food standards are similar. Their standards of dress vary little. All live at the bottom of the economic scale, upon small incomes, with little or no margin.

How much income do the Southern Negro land workers receive?

The United States Department of Agriculture in its monthly survey, *Crops and Markets*, for April, 1928, reports the wages of hired farm labor by states. The tables do not separate white and colored labor but the Department notes that "wage rates of the Southern States, especially of the South Central and particularly of the South Atlantic, reflect the low wage rates given Negroes." (Letter of June 13, 1928.)

Department of Agriculture figures give wage rates by the day and the month, with and without board.

Monthly farm wages with board in the North Atlantic

States and the East North Central States are fairly uniform. In the North Atlantic States they range from $37.50 per month in Pennsylvania to $55 per month in Rhode Island. In the North Central States, the minimum was reported from Missouri: $33.50 per month; the maximum from Iowa: $48.25 per month. The same uniformity holds true in the South Atlantic and South Central States. But the income levels are far different. Farm wages in the Northern States are almost twice as high as they are in the Southern States.

Farm wages, per month, with board, averaged $45.05 per month in the North Atlantic States; $41.38 per month in the North Central States. In the South, wages averaged $24.89 per month in the South Atlantic States and $24.88 per month in the South Central States. Monthly wage rates with board in the Western States were $53.10—well above those of the North and more than twice the rates for the South.

The South, in so far as farm wages are concerned, is in a class by itself—far below the level for the remainder of the country. This low wage standard represents the low economic standard of the Negro mass land workers.

There is some variation in farm wages from one Southern state to another. Thus, in Delaware and Maryland farm labor received respectively $31 and $36 per month with board. Labor in these states is chiefly engaged in raising truck for Northern markets. In South Carolina and Georgia, on the other hand, farm labor received $20 and $19.75 per month respectively. These are two of the principal cotton growing states.

The same low standard appears in the Gulf States: Alabama, $21 per month; Mississippi, $22.25; Louisiana, $22.75. It is in these states, from South Carolina to Louisiana, that the heart of the Black Belt lies. It is in these states, from South Carolina to Mississippi, that farm wages are half the Northern rate and less than 40 percent of the Western rate. It is in these states that the depressing influence of Negro mass labor on the general wage level is most manifest.

According to the Department of Agriculture figures, in the spring of 1928 there were eight Southern States in which the average monthly wage, with board, was less than $25. In one state—Georgia—the rate fell below $20.

By inference these wage rates of farm labor represent the approximate income level of the masses of Southern Negro land workers. If the croppers made incomes notably larger than those of the farm hands, the latter would be pushing into the cropper class. If, on the other hand, the farm hands made much better incomes than the croppers, the croppers would become farm hands. Where movement of labor from one group to another is easy, the level of incomes quickly adjusts itself.

Therefore, these Department of Agriculture figures probably give a fair picture of income among Southern land workers. The direct consequences of these low income rates appear in the form of bad diet and meager housing.

Earnings of Southern Negro women and children are correspondingly low. The Children's Bureau has conducted a series of investigations in various parts of the South. In the oyster and shrimp canning communities along the Gulf Coast 115 Negro women reported weekly earnings ranging from $1 to $12.50. Twenty-nine and five-tenths percent of the women reported wages of less than $4 per week; 48.7 percent reported wages of from $4 to $7.50 per week; 21.8 percent earned more than $7.50 per week. These wages were, of course, without board. (Paradise, *Oyster and Shrimp Canning Communities*, p. 55.)

Many Negro children work for hire on the land. The Children's Bureau in two bulletins, *Child Labor and the Work of Mothers on Gulf Truck Farms*, Washington, 1924, and *Child Labor on Maryland Truck Farms*, Washington, 1923, made special studies of the conditions surrounding working children. In the Maryland study the investigators found, in the Negro families studied, 322 children who did field work. Twenty-six of these children, 8.1 percent, were under 8 years of age; 65, 20.2 percent, were from 8 to 10, 77, 23.9 percent, were from 10 to 12 years of age; 46.9 percent were over 12. (*Child Labor on Maryland Truck Farms*, p. 8.)

Much of the field work, particularly that done by women and children, is piece work and highly seasonal, depending on the time of the year, on the weather, and on the state of the crop. The workers are paid only when they work and then on a piece rate basis.

The purchasing power of income is considerably greater in the South than in the North and is larger in country districts than in industrial areas.

Standard of living studies have not been made in the South as they have in the North. While no direct comparison is possible, the facts may be contrasted.

Family living for a man, wife and three children has been estimated for Northern industrial communities at from $2,160 to $2,622 per year ($180 to $218 per month). The amount varies with the size of the community. The smaller figure refers to small industrial cities. These amounts—$180 to $218 per month—will provide "health and decency" for a family of five. The food item alone in these budgets, is from $65 to $95 per month. (*American Labor Year Book*, 1927, p. 38.)

Wages of Southern farm hands by the month, without board, for April, 1928, averaged just over $35.

They were $52.75 in Maryland; $47 in West Virginia; $45 in Delaware; $41 in Virginia; $42.50 in Oklahoma; $40 in Texas. No state in the heart of the Black Belt reported monthly wages for farm hands of more than $37. The rate in North Carolina was $37; Kentucky, $36.50; Louisiana, $34.75; Florida, $34.50; Arkansas, $34.50; Tennessee, $33; Mississippi, $31.50. Finally there were three states which reported monthly farm hand wages, without board, at less than $30 per month: Alabama, $29; Georgia, $28; South Carolina, $27.75. The bottom of the scale was therefore touched in Georgia and South Carolina.

Taking the average monthly wage for the South of $35 and assuming steady work, a field hand would earn $390 per year. In Alabama, Georgia and South Carolina, field hands, assuming steady work, would earn less than $350 per year.

These earnings do not represent total family income. The wages of the men are so low that women and children are compelled to supplement them by working for wages wherever possible. Furthermore, in these Southern agricultural communities, rents are very cheap, and the families are able to eke out part of their existence by raising vegetables, chickens, pigs. Still, where all allowances have been made for work by all available members of the family and for supplementary income derived from the kitchen garden, the wage rates of agricultural workers in the South are so low that by no wildest stretch of the imagination could they be described as "health and decency" wages. Thirty dollars a month, for an able bodied man, with prices at their present level, is less than a family subsistence wage.

Negro women are reported in the Occupations Census as being gainfully employed in a much larger percentage of cases than white women. The reason is obvious.

◆ 57 ◆

The wages of Negro men compel the women to earn a share of family income.

Southern farm wages and incomes yield less than subsistence. They are so low as to preclude the possibility of even a wholesome diet and decent clothing, without taking any account of the cultural side of life.

8: LIVING CONDITIONS

LIVING conditions of Southern Negroes, particularly those working on the land, may be characterized under three heads: housing, education and social opportunity. In all three directions the position of the Southern Negro is greatly inferior to that of the Southern white.

Negro housing in the South is generally inadequate. The Negro shanties, built of logs in a few cases and of wood in most instances, are usually unpainted, old, out of repair, squalid, lacking modern conveniences, un-supplied with the simplest necessaries such as running water, adequate toilet facilities, heating facilities and the like.

Paul Blanshard writes of the Southern mill village (*Labor in Southern Cotton Mills*, pp. 67-68):

> "At the edge of many of the Southern mill villages is nigger town, a short stretch of road flanked by small, unpainted cottages which have the general appearance of being run down at the heels. Its houses are usually without lights and running water."

Children's Bureau investigators give a similar report concerning the oyster and shrimp canning communities along the Gulf Coast:

> "The Negro districts presented in general a par-ticularly ramshackle appearance. They were often situated along the railroad tracks or in swampy, isolated districts. . . . The streets, even when the district was near the center of the city, were seldom paved, nor were the roads kept in good condition.

Yet, despite the loose boards, the sagging porches, and the general disrepair of the gray, weather-beaten houses, tiny, neat, well-kept gardens which were the rule rather than the exception, gave to the district a cheerful air. . . ." (Paradise *Oyster and Shrimp Canning Communities on the Gulf Coast*, pp. 81-82.)

Another Children's Bureau study, *The Welfare of Children in Cotton Growing Areas of Texas*, gives this description of Negro housing in two Texas cotton raising counties:

"Among Negro families, the three or four room house was the most common. Practically all were one story, frame buildings, with no basement and no foundation other than pillars or wooden blocks. Few houses had any modern conveniences. In Hill County most of them were heated by stoves, but in Rusk County, 89 percent of the white and 82 percent of the Negro families visited depended upon a fire-place for heating. . . . Among Negro families in Rusk County only 7 percent, and only 2 percent of the Negro families in Hill County, reported water in the house or on the porch. None of the Negro families in either county had a sink." (Pp. 38-39.)

These are typical instances that give a fair picture of the housing of the Southern Negro masses who live on the land and in the Southern communities. Negro housing in the South is antiquated, inadequate, unsanitary and wretched.

Education is a second and very important phase of living conditions. Relatively little money is spent in the South for the education of Negroes.

Expenditures for educational purposes are given by the Commission on Inter-racial Cooperation, Atlanta, Georgia, in its report, *Race Relations in 1927.*

AVERAGE ANNUAL EXPENDITURES
PER CHILD OF SCHOOL AGE

	For Whites	For Negroes
Alabama	$26.57	$ 3.81
Arkansas	13.36	6.48
Florida	42.01	7.33
Georgia	25.84	5.78
Louisiana	33.73	5.48
Mississippi	25.95	5.62
North Carolina	25.31	7.52
South Carolina	27.88	2.74
Tennessee	21.02	11.88
Texas	31.77	20.24
Virginia	40.27	10.47

These figures indicate that under the most favorable conditions, prevailing, for example, in Tennessee and Texas, the average annual expenditure for education per child of school age is about half as great for Negro children as it is for white children. Under less favorable circumstances, such as those prevailing in Georgia, Florida, Mississippi, Louisiana, North Carolina and Virginia, expenditure per child of school age is four, five or six times as great for white children as it is for colored children. In South Carolina expenditures for white children of school age are almost exactly ten times as great as for colored children of school age.

Numerous studies and comments have been made on the educational discrimination which is systematically carried on against the Negro and in favor of the white throughout the South. With segregated schools and with inadequate school funds, Negro boys and girls are fortunate if they are able to attend the elementary schools. High school and college training is beyond the reach of the vast majority.

The Children's Bureau in its study of Texas cotton growing areas found half of the Negro children in Hill County and one-sixth of the children in Rusk County not attending school. (*Welfare of Children in Cotton Growing Areas of Texas*, pp. 76-77.) Other Children's Bureau studies indicate that where the Negro children work as field hands, school attendance invariably suffers.

The educational situation in the South is thus summed up by T. J. Woofter, Jr. (*Negro Problems in Cities*, p. 201):

> "School funds are not adequate to meet the needs either in the North or in the South. The South, however, is not only poorer than the North but also less disposed to distribute such funds as are available according to the school population. The Negro schools are a secondary consideration. In comparison with schools for white children they have fewer seats in proportion to the school population, more pupils per teacher, more double sessions, fewer teachers, poorer salaries, fewer and smaller playgrounds, and less adequate provision for the health and comfort of pupils and teachers."

The *Crisis* for September, 1926 (p. 254), publishes the following analysis of school expenditures in Bibb County, Georgia:

1. No. of Children 6 to 18 years of age—1923
   White 10,642
   Colored 8,847
2. Disbursements for 1923
   a. Teachers—White $320,868.66
      Teachers—Colored 52,292.00

b. Buildings and Repairs
   White 16,941.29
   Colored ....
c. Equipment—White 3,127.57
   Equipment—Colored ....
d. Supplies, Libraries, Jani-
   tors, Fuel and Other Ex-
   penditures
   White 85,344.27
   Colored ....
e. Transportation—White .. 14,969.93
   Transportation—Colored   ....

The same number of the *Crisis* published statistics for Glynn County and Ware County, Georgia, which shows substantially the same situation as that existing in Bibb County.

This report on education in Georgia was the result of a careful first-hand study made by the National Association for the Advancement of Colored People. On pages 263-264 the following summary of the survey appears:

"First, it does not appear that the colored schools enter definitely into the minds of those who are charged with common school education. . . .

"The data collected from counties scattered over the State show that in fifteen counties the schools run less than 6 months, which is the legal requirement. The churches and lodge rooms which are used for Negro schools are chiefly old, dilapidated buildings, unfit for teaching purposes. In some cases, they have no means of getting light; often there are no desks. In most of the churches and lodge halls, the children sit on plank benches which sometimes have no backs to them. In some counties there is not a single school building for colored children.

"The fact that there is great hostility towards Negro education is attested by the burning of schools in several sections. Two instances are recited in our survey. . . .

"When we consider the salary paid Negro teachers we find it as low as $15 per month in some places. The salaries are often supplemented by ten and fifteen cents per pupil, which is paid by the patrons."

Opportunities for the higher education of Negroes are even less abundant than those for elementary education. Educationally the South punishes children who are born black.

Little need be said about the social position of the Southern Negro. He is a field hand. He is a servant. Even where he has become a skilled mechanic, a business man or a professional man, he is treated as though he were still doing menial work. The Negro, in the South, is a member of a subject, exploited race, universally denied equality with the whites. Negro children grow up with the fact of their inferiority constantly thrown in their faces.

Southern Negroes are surrounded by an atmosphere of racial antagonism, hatred and threatened conflict. Economic, political and social discrimination against Negroes is met with at every turn. The Negro is the object of ridicule, attack, assault, murder. If he attempts to fight back, there is a race war. Working conditions in the South are disadvantageous to the Negro. Living conditions are such that the Negro in his housing, in education, in his social opportunity, is in a position of constant racial inferiority.

9: CENTERS OF ECONOMIC POWER

TEN million Negroes live in a dozen Southern states. Sixty-five years ago their ancestors were slaves in these same states. Then, as now, the centers of Southern economic power were in the hands of the whites.

When the emancipation of the slaves was proclaimed in 1863 the number of slave-holding families was about 350,000. The number of slaves was at least four million. Thus the average number of slaves per slave-holding family was in the neighborhood of 12. In slave days a very small minority of Southern whites owned and exploited a vast army of Southern blacks. Today the descendants of those slave-holding whites own the land and capital with which the descendants of those Negro slaves must work in order to live.

Under the slave system the centers of Southern economic power lay in the cotton, tobacco, sugar and rice plantations. Under the new economic order which has arisen from the ruins of the slave system, the centers of Southern economic power lie in two directions. On the one hand there are the railroads, the industries, the mines, the banks, the public utilities, the insurance and merchandising that make up Southern business enterprise. On the other hand is the cultivation of cotton, sugar, tobacco, rice, corn and other Southern agricultural staples.

Negroes, in states such as Mississippi, Georgia and South Carolina, make up approximately half of the total population. In the other Southern States the proportion of Negroes in the population is a quarter or two-fifths. To what extent do Negroes own, control or direct the economic life in communities of which they form so large a part?

The question cannot be answered statistically, save for farm ownership. There are no adequate figures showing the distribution of stocks, bonds, mortgages and title deeds by race.

A visitor to the centers of Southern economic enterprise does not require statistics in order to realize the complete domination of the whites. It is merely necessary to pass through corporation offices; to read the names of boards of directors; to attend conventions of men in various leading business lines; to dine in business clubs. The industrialists of the South are white, almost to a man.

Southern railroad and public utilities are owned chiefly by the whites. Control is exclusively in their hands. They are the directors, the executives, the managers. They decide policy, and direct organization. Tens of thousands of Negroes are employed on Southern railroads. Most of them work as laborers in maintenance and construction crews. A few hold skilled positions. There the story ends. Negroes do not advance "from the ranks" to shape the destiny of Southern railroad enterprise. The South is a white man's country where Negroes work under white supervision.

Southern manufacturing industries are also under white domination. The iron and steel industry with its subsidiaries, the textile industry, the tobacco industry, are almost completely controlled by white enterprise. In many Southern industrial plants Negroes do not work at all, except in menial capacities. Laws, in some of the Southern States, require separate workrooms for Negroes, and thus practically exclude them from establishments in which white workers are employed. As industrialization has proceeded in the South, the whites have monopolized not only the executive posts and the skilled and highly paid trades. They have have also held the run of factory jobs.

Occasionally Negro management has made attempts to enter the industrial field, raising capital among Negroes and employing Negro labor. The instances are rare enough to excite newspaper comment. Almost uniformly they have failed after a very brief existence, leaving manufacturing in the hands of the whites.

Negro business men may be found in all parts of the South—running groceries, selling vegetables, conducting restaurants, hotels, barber-shops. There are Negro builders and contractors, Negro insurance men, Negro newspaper and magazine managers, Negro printers. Negroes have entered many other occupations in the fields of trade and service.

Two matters are worthy of note in this connection: first, these Negro business men are usually not engaged in any basic industry. Steel, lumber, textile, tobacco are entirely out of their field. Second, they usually serve Negroes. In many cases their patronage is exclusively Negro. Negroes have not penetrated the major industrial enterprises of the South. Even wholesale merchandising remains with the whites. The businesses in which they are active lie on the fringe of the business world.

Banking is a function of the Southern whites. That, of course, is one of the reasons why major Negro enterprises have not been more successful. The Negro has been compelled to go to white bankers for his line of credit. Southern white bankers do not manage their banks for the purpose of pushing Negroes forward along lines of major business enterprise, and there are few Negro bankers to whom Negro business men can turn. Until the World War era, Negroes had scarcely entered the banking field.

Furthermore, Southern banking and business enterprise have been directly allied with Northern banking and business enterprise. Though it is no longer true that Southern business is chiefly dependent on Northern business, the post Civil War development of the South was pushed forward and financed in large part from the North. In those days, even more than today, Northern business was exclusively in the hands of the whites.

Neither in the South nor in the North could Negro business men get adequate credit. As in every other important field, banking was a white man's world to which Negroes were only grudgingly and occasionally admitted.

Free Negroes in the South, long before the Civil War, were engaged in many lines of small scale business enterprise. Today they occupy many of the same fields. Negroes who engage in Southern business are in areas of secondary importance. They have not touched basic business enterprise. In the less strategic business fields, suffering all of the disabilities that go with membership in an inferior, subject race, Negroes enjoy meager opportunities in retail trade, in service to Negroes, in furthering Negro enterprise.

The strategic centers of Southern economic power—railroading, textile, steel, lumber, manufacturing, building, banking are occupied by Southern white men. Merchandising is also largely in their hands.

One field the Negroes have entered—the field of land ownership. The Census of 1920 reported 159,651 Negro farmers who owned their farms in full. In a few sections they actually control better land and make more profits from their land than do the competing whites. This is exceptional, however. Most of the Southern land is in the control of the white race. The Agricultural Census of 1925 reported 3,131,418 farms in the South. Of these farms 831,455 were operated by Negroes and 2,299,963 by whites. Even where Negroes have made the most progress, the Southern whites dominate the economic situation. They are the owning class.

Most Southern Negroes work on land owned and controlled by white farmers. There were 636,248 Negro tenant farmers in the South when the Agricultural Census of 1925 was taken. Practically all the land farmed by these tenants was owned by whites. The Census of 1920 reported 1,192,504 Negroes occupied as wage workers on farms. Since nine-tenths of the Negroes in the North and West live in cities, these Negro agricultural wage workers must have been employed almost entirely in the Southern States. (The Census does not make the separation by race and by states.) The great majority of these Negroes worked for white employers. Out of five Southern Negro farm operators, four are tenants. Out of ten Southern Negroes occupied in gaining a living on the land, eight or nine are directly dependent on the whites for their livelihood.

Most of the Southern blacks work on land owned by Southern whites. Sometimes they work as tenant farmers; sometimes as wage workers. In either case they are economically at the mercy of white exploiters.

Negroes have done more in the field of land ownership than in any other field to break through the restrictive cordon of economic control which the Southern white race has built around the Southern Negroes from the early days of slavery. Even in land ownership, however, the Negroes have barely made a beginning.

Economic power in the North rests as a matter of course in the hands of the whites. Negroes make up only one-fortieth of the Northern population. They play practically no part in the direction of Northern economic life.

Economic power in the South is also in white hands. Negroes are relatively few in the North. In the South they are numerous. Occasionally they make up a majority of the population. Nowhere, however, do they exercise a majority or even a considerable minority of economic control.

The authority of any ruling class rests upon its economic power. The masters of feudal Europe ruled because (and where) they held the land. They made every effort to keep the land in a comparatively few hands because they realized that the land-holding class was bound to be the ruling class. The masters of present-day industry rule because (and where) they own stocks, bonds, mortgages, title deeds. They make every effort to keep this ownership in their own hands because they realize that the capital-holding class is bound to be the ruling class. When dealing with a subject, exploited race, like the Negroes, the members of the white owning class are particularly careful to prevent members of the exploited race from becoming exploiters. This not only breaks the monopoly of the exploiting whites, but "spoils" the exploited blacks for further exploitation. The whites therefore spare no means to keep the centers of economic power under their exclusive control.

Economic power in the United States remains a function of the white race. It is a field of activity from which Negroes are almost completely excluded, or into which they have thus far failed to penetrate. The white ruling class of the United States, South as well as North, remains economically supreme. The citadel of ruling class authority—property ownership—and the source of ruling class profit—job control—are in white hands.

10: THE NEGRO GOES TO TOWN

THE typical Negro slave was a worker on a Southern plantation. Until about 1900 the typical American Negro was still a field-hand or servant in one of a dozen Southern states where rice, sugar, tobacco, corn and cotton are the staple crops. Recently there has been a rapid movement of Negroes away from the farms to the industrial centers, and away from the South to the North and West.

The American Negro migration of the twentieth century is part of a world-wide movement away from the land. This movement has been felt particularly in those countries which were passing through a process of rapid industrialization. Its basic cause lies in the very great increase in economic and social advantages which the farm worker is able to enjoy when he succeeds in getting skilled or semi-skilled work in an industrial center. White farmers as well as Negro farmers have taken part in this movement in the United States.

Between 1910 and 1920 the rural Negro population of the United States actually decreased 3.4 percent. During the same ten years, the urban Negro population increased 32.6 percent. In 1920 there were 224,876 fewer Negroes living in rural communities than in 1910. In 1920 there were 870,244 more Negroes living in urban communities than in 1910. These figures indicate a migration on a vast scale.

The shift was stimulated by the war, although it was not confined to the war period. Negro urban dwellers numbered 1.5 million in 1890; 2 million in 1900; 3.5 million in 1920. The movement to the city has been going on for decades.

Proportionately there has been a steady increase in

city-dwelling Negroes. Nineteen and four-tenths percent of the American Negroes lived in cities in 1890; in
1900 the percentage of city dwellers was 22.7 percent;
in 1910, 27.4 percent, and in 1920, 34 percent.

This movement from country to city was not confined to the Negroes. It affected the whole population
of the United States. Between 1900 and 1910 the white
population in cities increased faster than the Negro
population. Between 1910 and 1920, however, the
Negro population in cities increased more rapidly than
the white population in cities. This was due in part to
the check of immigration and in part to the very rapid
increase in Negro migration during the latter period.

Negro migrants from country to city have not all
come north. The Negro population of many southern
cities has increased as rapidly as the Negro population
in northern cities with corresponding industrial opportunities. The Negro population of New York, for example, increased 51 percent between 1900 and 1910 and
66 percent between 1910 and 1920. The Negro population of Philadelphia increased 35 percent between
1900 and 1910 and 59 percent between 1910 and 1920.
In Chicago, the Negro population increased 46 percent
between 1900 and 1910 and 148 percent between 1910
and 1920. In Detroit it increased 40 percent between
1900 and 1910 and 611 percent between 1910 and 1920.
In Birmingham, Alabama, it increased 215 percent between 1900 and 1910 and 34 percent between 1910 and
1920. Norfolk, Virginia, increased its Negro population 24 percent between 1900 and 1910 and 73 percent
between 1910 and 1920. The Negroes in Jacksonville,
Florida, increased 80 percent between 1900 and 1910
and 42 percent between 1910 and 1920. Negroes are
leaving the country for the city—South as well as
North.

Basically the Negro migration is a movement from

the farm to the factory—from the country to the city. Incidentally it is a movement from the South to the North. The East South Central States with a total Negro population in 1910 of 2,652,000 reported an actual loss by 1920 of 4 percent. The South Atlantic States with a total Negro population of 4,081,000 in 1910 reported an increase during the following decade of only 5 percent. The West South Central States in the same period showed an increase in the Negro population of 4 percent. During the same ten years the increase in Negro population in the New England States was 19 percent; for the Middle Atlantic States, 40 percent; and for the East North Central States, 71 percent. While the great mass of Negroes remained in the South, their proportionate increases were far greater in the North.

The Negroes who came North came to the cities. The Census of 1920 showed that while for the United States as a whole 34 percent of the Negroes lived in urban communities, in New England the percentage was 90; in the Middle Atlantic States, 86 percent and in the East North Central States, 87 percent. This territory, stretching from the Atlantic Ocean to the Mississippi Valley, contains the bulk of United States heavy industry. Since the majority of Northern Negroes live in these three sections of the United States, the Northern migration of the Negroes has been almost entirely a migration to Northern cities.

While the latest census was taken in 1920, subsequent estimates of Negro population in Northern cities show a continuation of the migratory movement. The Urban League of Chicago estimates the Negro population of that city as 43,000 in 1910; 109,000 in 1920 and 165,-000 in 1928. For Detroit the Urban League estimates of Negro population are: for 1910, 5,741; for 1921, 41,533; and for 1928, 86,000. The Negro population of Philadelphia, according to estimates made by the Armstrong Association, was 89,000 in 1915; 134,000 in 1920 and 175,000 in 1928. The Negro population of Los Angeles was estimated by the Urban League at 1,258 in 1890; 2,131 in 1900; 7,599 in 1910 and 15,579 in 1920. Similar studies in other Northern cities show corresponding increases in the Negro population.

Charles S. Johnson, Research Director of the Urban League, estimates that between 1916 and 1928, 1,200,-000 Negroes migrated from the South to the North. Perhaps 200,000 of these returned South, leaving a net total migration for the twelve years of about one million. If these estimates are correct, within a decade a tenth of the whole Negro population of the South has come North, chiefly to Northern cities. Since correspondingly large numbers of Negroes have gone into Southern cities, the disrupting effect upon Southern rural life and upon the Southern rural labor market can be readily imagined.

The total number of Negroes living in the North in 1870 was 452,818. Missouri, however, reported 118,071 of this Negro population and Missouri is essentially a Southern state. In the same year, Pennsylvania had a Negro population of 65,294; Ohio, of 62,213; New York, 52,081; New Jersey, 30,658; Illinois, 28,762, and Indiana, 24,560. There was no other Northern state with a Negro population of 15,000.

By comparison, in 1920, there were 1,472,000 Negroes in the North. Pennsylvania reported a Negro population of 284,578; New York, 194,483; Ohio, 186,187; Illinois, 182,272; Indiana, 80,810. Eight Northern states contained four-fifths of the total Northern Negro population. With the exception of Michigan and New York these eight states all bordered on the South.

Evidently, therefore, during recent years Negro population has been moving out of the Black Belt into the cities of the border states and into certain other cities, like New York and Detroit, that offer unusual industrial opportunities or social attractions.

The economic position of the Southern Negro masses never has been very good. In recent years it has grown notably worse. First came the boll weevil, wiping out the cotton raising industry in many parts of the South and ruining hundreds of thousands of cotton growers. Then floods. Finally, after the war, the dramatic collapse in the prices of all staple farm products.

The war intensified racial and other discriminations all over the United States. Incidental to the war came the demand for labor in the North, with the extensive Negro migrations of 1916 and 1917. Southern planters and business men, seeing their labor supply slipping away and finding themselves forced by competition with Northern labor markets to pay higher wages to Southern Negro labor, resorted to terroristic methods in order to hold the Negroes in the South. This combination of forces merely served to stimulate Negro migration.

The unskilled Southern Negro farm hand could go into a Southern or Northern industrial town and receive wages considerably higher than those being paid on the farm. To be sure, his living costs were increased, but if he left his family in the South, where living costs were cheaper, and lived economically himself in some Northern industrial center, the money which he could earn would go much further toward family support than the income which he would have secured had he remained on the land. Wesley notes that male farm laborers in 1916 were getting from 50 to 75 cents per day. Some Georgia farm hands were working for from $10 to $12 per month. In the Southern cities unskilled Negro workers were earning from $1 to $1.50 per day; skilled workers from $2 to $3.50 per day. "In the

North these figures were doubled, and in the case of farm hands, trebled." (Wesley, *Negro Labor in the United States*, p. 293.)

Northern cities offered the Southern Negro a chance of rising economically. Negro centers were growing rapidly in all of the principal Northern industrial areas. Negro lawyers, doctors, dentists, real estate men and insurance men had an exceptional chance to establish themselves in these rapidly growing Northern Negro colonies. Such opportunities led to the migration of Southern Negro business and professional men to take advantage of the new professional opportunities in the North.

Cultural opportunitites were also greater in the North. Grade schools were better. There were high schools and professional schools to which Negro boys and girls could go. Cultural contacts were possible not only within the Negro colonies, but with certain elements in the white population as well. The Negro was more free than he had been in the South.

Industrial society offers material rewards far richer than those which agricultural society can afford. American Negroes, confined until recent years to farm or domestic labor, have entered the industrial field as active competitors with whites in all parts of the United States. No longer are they content with pork, corn-bread and molasses in a shanty on a Southern plantation. They have heard and seen what chances there are for material and cultural well-being in the great centers of steel and concrete that are the core of American urban life. Now they propose to enjoy some of the good things that modern life has to offer.

11: JOB FINDING FOR NEGROES

NEGROES who leave cotton fields and sugar plantations for centers of industry must find jobs. On the land of the South the mass of Negro field workers comes into competition with the whites only incidentally. In the industrial centers they are still a tiny minority that must fight with the whites for every inch of advance in economic opportunity.

As slaves Negroes were expected to do all kinds of work. Here, too, their competition with whites was slight.

Negro slaves were frequently trained as blacksmiths, sawmill hands, carpenters, bricklayers, plasterers, wheelwrights, shoemakers, millers, bakers, tanners, shipwrights. Slave owners not only trained their Negro bondsmen for these professions, but they frequently rented them out for long periods. Before the abolition of slavery Negro artisans were replacing white artisans throughout the South.

When the Negroes were emancipated they were forced to compete with white workers. So long as they were willing to remain on the plantations and to do the housework, this competition was not particularly sharp. When they entered the field of industry with its higher rewards and greater economic opportunities, competition with white labor became savage.

Industrialization followed the abolition of slavery in the South. The Southern whites, former slave owners and mountaineers alike, were drawn into the industrial vortex. At the same time that the emancipated Negroes were seeking industrial opportunity, the whites were entering the competitive struggle for the control of the new economic system.

The whites won—easily. Then they closed the door of industrial opportunity to the Negro.

Negroes had been building workers, mechanics, artisans, craftsmen. As factory industry replaced hand labor, the strategic and the best paying among these occupations were preempted by the whites.

From certain occupations in the industrial field, the Negroes have been almost entirely excluded. White collar jobs are generally denied to Negroes. Jessie O. Thomas writing on "Economic Deadlines in the South" (*Opportunity*, February, 1926, p. 49), states: "There is probably not a Negro bookkeeper, stenographer, 'honest-to-goodness' clerk in the whole South, employed other than by his own race; not a Negro supervisor in the Post Office, for however long the Negro may work in the Post Office and regardless of how efficient he may be, he does not get beyond the position of clerk; no street car conductors or motormen, telephone and switchboard operators."

The same general situation prevails in the Border States and in the North. "Who would expect to find a Negro clerk in a white man's store or a Negro bookkeeper or stenographer in a white man's office is surely not acquainted with the conditions in the North today," writes H. G. Duncan. (*Changing Race Relationships*, p. 77.) A Negro answered an ad for a position as clerk in the suburbs of Philadelphia. "What do you suppose we'd want of a Negro?" was the question with which the store-keeper met him. (*Idem.*)

In a number of Northern cities Business Colleges refuse to accept Negro students. Business Schools of St. Paul, Minnesota, formerly accepted Negro students. Recently the schools have refused Negro students as the office managers of St. Paul will not employ Negro bookkeepers, stenographers or clerks.

"Negro girls were formerly employed in offices here,"

said a representative of the St. Paul Urban League. "Now they are universally refused. There are no colored sales girls in stores. They work there only as maids and attendants. A Negro girl cannot get a sales job or a clerical job here unless she is fair enough to pass as white."

One of the leading Negroes of New Haven, Connecticut, said: "We turn out Negro girls from the schools each year who are well qualified to do office and sales work. They can find little or nothing to do.

"There is no room for them in offices.

"Stores never give them a chance behind the counter. They can sweep and dust and act as maids. But for those jobs no school training is necessary."

Stores are particularly strict in their exclusion of Negro sales people.

A Negro woman, graduate of a Southern College, applied for a job in a Chicago department store. She was very fair, and as she did not state that she was a Negro, the employment department never suspected it. Within two months this woman had the best sales record of any one in the department. At the end of four years, she stood out as one of the most efficient saleswomen in the entire store.

One morning she was called into the manager's office at three minutes of nine. At two minutes after nine she was leaving the store—dismissed. The management had discovered that the woman was of Negro extraction.

Manufacturing establishments frequently follow a policy of excluding Negroes from ordinary factory employment. An Urban League survey of Fort Wayne, Indiana, made in 1928, showed that among the 11 largest industrial plants in the city, 4 employed no Negroes, 3 employed a total of 7 Negroes, and the remaining 4 employed 220 Negroes. The total number of white employees in these eleven plants was 17,334.

The plants included an electric manufacturing concern, with 5,759 workers and 3 Negroes; a knitting mill with 1,504 workers and no Negroes; an agricultural implement plant with 1,400 workers and 54 Negroes, a railroad shop with 2,070 workers and 70 Negroes, a foundry with 379 workers and 31 Negroes, and a rolling mill with 315 workers and 65 Negroes.

Several careful industrial surveys made by the Urban League show a sharp division of policy between employers on the question of employing Negro labor. In many important plants Negro workers are excluded merely because "we don't hire Negro help."

Generally where Negroes are hired they do the dirty work. Charles S. Johnson reports in his Urban League Industrial Survey of Los Angeles, "Negroes are associated, traditionally, with . . . domestic service, and, in some instances, common labor. Actually the bulk of them are engaged in these two lines." In Philadelphia, the Armstrong Association reports the employment of 300 Negroes by one of the leading department stores of the city. They are elevator operators, maids, or stock girls, but they do not occupy clerical or sales positions. Negroes are employed very little in the principal machine shops and in the textile factories. On the street-railways a number of Negroes occupy positions as foremen, but in general they do the common labor work. They are never employed as conductors or motormen. In the principal railroad offices "responsible jobs are not open to them. In one railroad office where Negroes have long been employed as messengers, they are now being replaced by young white men."

An investigator from Baltimore reports that Negroes are excluded almost wholly from highly skilled operations. There are no Negro registered plumbers or electricians in Baltimore. Negro linotypers are admitted grudgingly. There are less than a dozen Negro movie operators. In the clothing industry Negroes are employed, but the strongest group of Negro workers in Baltimore is among the longshoremen. This Negro Longshoremen's Union has forty years of history behind it. No Negroes are employed on the street cars of Baltimore, but they do work for the street railway company on repair gangs, as car cleaners, and in other inferior positions.

An Urban League post-war survey of Buffalo gives a very complete occupational classification of Negro men:

	Total Number of Workers	Negro
Skilled	54,336	332
Laborers	25,189	798
Semi-Skilled	17,260	183
General Workers	5,111	35
Personal and Domestic	8,174	81
Clerical Workers	20,618	43
Work Requiring Examinations	4,047	8
Business Men	14,939	27
Public Service	834	7
Professional Service	7,292	57
Apprentices	1,554	1
Foremen and Superintendents	8,017	11

United States railroads employ 136,065 Negroes of whom about three-fourths are laborers and one-seventh porters. The remaining Negro workers are widely distributed over various railway occupations. Half of these Negro railway workers are employed in eight Southern States. (Wesley, *Negro Labor in the United States*, pp. 301-2.)

An Indianapolis employer summed up the position of the Negro in these words: "Negroes get only the left-over jobs—the hard manual work. They are employed to do some of the more disagreeable jobs in the stock yards; they get the heaviest tasks in the factories. They do not hold either the nice jobs or the important jobs anywhere. I have employed two Chinese and a Hindu. As yet I have never dared to employ a colored man about the factory."

This employer stated that the situation of the Negro in Indianapolis was much worse since the War of 1914 with its accompanying migration. The rapid increase in the number of Negroes in the city led to sharp competition between Negroes and whites and the tenser race feeling which this competition generated.

Until 1914 Negroes were practically excluded from responsible industrial positions. The war gave them their first great industrial opportunity. Widespread strikes from 1919 to 1922 enlarged that opportunity by making it possible for Negroes to enter industries from which they had formerly been practically excluded and to secure skilled jobs which up to that time had been wholly monopolized by white workers.

The war stimulated production. At the same time it limited immigration. The only considerable source of mass labor in America was the Negro population. It was this combination of circumstances that enabled the Negroes from 1915 to 1922 to break into essentially new industrial fields.

Up to the period of the war trade schools, with minor exceptions, had taken few Negro students. Their reason was the obvious impossibility of placing trained Negro workers. Professional education for Negroes was even more limited. The pioneer work of certain Negro educational institutions was supplying a considerable number of Negro artisans and Negro professionals. War demand quickly absorbed this supply and led to the rapid enlargement of educational facilities. In the same way war wages made it possible for Negro parents to increase the number of opportunities that they could offer their children.

The Urban League in its Industrial Survey of Trenton reports an investigation made in that city in 1902 in which out of 398 establishments, with a total of 128,412 employees only 83 establishments employed Negroes in any capacity. This was typical of the industrial position of Negroes throughout the United States.

Within the next twenty years profound changes took place. The United States Census of 1920 reported Negroes in a wide range of industrial activity: 9,046 blacksmiths; 1,402 boilermakers; 10,736 brick masons; 34,916 carpenters and cabinet makers; 19,849 cigar and tobacco workers; 3,596 clay, glass and stone workers; 13,888 clothing workers; 2,252 coopers; 27,160 dressmakers; 1,411 electricians; 6,353 stationary engineers and 29,640 firemen. The list extends to most of the principal manufacturing and mechanical occupations. In 1910, 406,582 Negroes were engaged in manufacturing and mechanical pursuits. Ten years later, the number was 566,680.

Occupational distribution of Negroes as shown by the Census of 1920 is analyzed in detail by E. B. Reuter. (*American Race Problems*, pp. 228 ff.) T. J. Woofter, Jr. summarizes the result of the Negro movement into industry in this way: "The most radical change caused by the movement since 1916 has been the entry of some 140,000 colored men into industry. These are, to a great extent, concentrated in eleven large industrial cities. The cities of Boston, New York, Philadelphia, Pittsburgh, Cleveland, Cincinnati, Detroit, Indianapolis, Chicago, St. Louis, Kansas City, include about 40 percent of all Negroes living outside of the South. In 1920, 230 plants employed some 115,000 of the 140,000 in manufacturing industries. According to industry, colored laborers in the North were distributed about as follows: iron and steel, 40,000; automobile, 25,000; meat packing, 15,000; Pullman shops and yards, 15,000; miscellaneous, 40,000." (Woofter, *Negro Migration*, p. 157.)

Trade union rules and exclusion from trade union bodies have proved to be an effective obstacle to the industrial advancement of Negro workers. Charles H. Wesley in his *Negro Labor in the United States* prints a long chapter (Chapter IX, "Organized Labor and the Negro") dealing in great detail with the relation between organized labor and the Negro. Theoretically, the American Federation of Labor has always stood for the inclusion of the Negro in the ranks of organized labor. Practically, while a small number of unions have excluded Negroes from membership by constitutional provision and by-laws, the great majority have simply refused to accept them when they applied for membership.

The American Negroes are industrially unskilled mass workers, confined to those jobs which pay the lowest wages and demand the heaviest work. Within the industries which do employ Negro labor, the line of separation between white man and black man is usually the line which separates highly paid, clean, comfortable jobs from low-paid, dirty, heavy work.

Until the World War the Negro freeman remained a field hand or a domestic worker. Within the last few years, however, he has launched a mass movement which aims to provide for the Negro worker an industrial opportunity equal to that of a white worker. Thus far in his job-seeking experiments the Negro has found the white man determined to keep black men in their places as hewers of wood and drawers of water.

2. Negro worker on construction job in Philadelphia.

1. Negro laborers doing construction work on Taylor Hotel, Akron, Ohio.

*3. A large amount of construction work in Washington
is performed by Negroes.*

4. Negro gang at work, Chestnut Street, Philadelphia.

5. Negroes lay a cement sidewalk in Washington.

6. Skilled Negro cement workers, Washington.

*7. Negro workers in Washington, D. C., relaying the
street railway.*

8. Negroes laying rails, Washington, D. C.

9. *Street paving work, Washington, D.C.*

10. *Negroes sifting sand for cement work, Washington, D.C.*

11. *Negro worker on street construction job, Washington, D. C.*

12. *Negro street worker, Washington, D. C.*

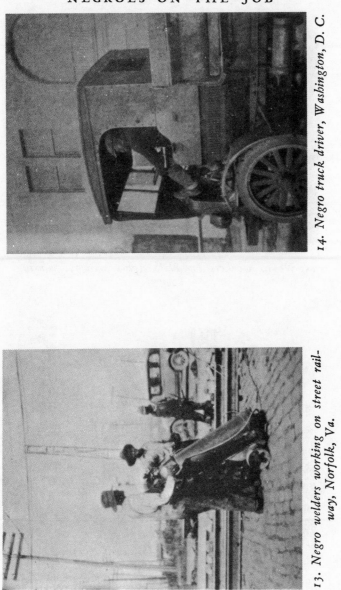

14. *Negro truck driver, Washington, D. C.*

13. *Negro welders working on street rail-way, Norfolk, Va.*

15. Negro workers on Philadelphia subway, pouring cement.

16. Negro worker handling rock from New York subway excavation.

18. *Philadelphia Negro subway worker.*

17. *Negro butcher, Hill District, Pittsburgh.*

19. Negro gang at work, Richmond, Va.

*20. Negro shovelers on the ore dumps of the Bethlehem
Steel Co., Sparrows Point, Md.*

21. Crew of Negro track workers, Norfolk, Va.

22. Negro laborers clearing up debris, building construction, Akron, Ohio.

23. *Negro paper gatherer, Philadelphia.*

24. *Negro iceman, Harlem, New York City.*

26. *Negro express handlers, Rocky Mount, N. C.*

25. *Negroes shifting mail sacks, Selma, N. C.*

27. Colored artisans in Newport News shipbuilding yards.

28. Negroes at work on a house-wrecking operation, Washington.

29. Negro workers on leather glazing machine, Chicago.

30. Negro women workers computing foot measurement of leather, Chicago.

31. *Negroes cutting and blending colors in beaver board factory, Chicago.*

32. *Negroes working on belt knife splitting machine, Chicago.*

12: ECONOMIC DISCRIMINATION

NEGROES who migrated from Southern farms have been able to penetrate only certain industrial fields. From the others they are excluded by the whites. Where they do penetrate they are discriminated against after they get their jobs.

The simplest economic discrimination is in the rate of pay.

Among white men, particularly where they are organized in trade unions, "equal pay for equal work" is accepted as an axiom. This is not so where Negroes and whites work together: on the contrary, there is persistent wage discrimination, though it is difficult to say how much.

Where Negroes and whites work together at hour rates they ordinarily receive the same wages, but in the distribution of work, foremen frequently give preference to the white workers.

Work which is distributed in the shop usually varies in character. This is particularly true of piece work. On such jobs the Negroes are frequently given the piece work on which the lowest wages can be made, while the whites get the better paying jobs. When there is a change in the character of operations new work goes to the Negroes while the whites retain the old jobs with which they are familiar and at which they can make higher rates than they would on the new operations.

In the needle trades the whites are given the finer work. Negro women make work shirts, overalls, button holes, and do other heavy and coarse work. The fine work, of course, pays better than the rough work.

Frequently, also, piece rates are so adjusted between the work that the whites are doing and the work that the

Negroes are doing that the whites are able to make better wages. W. D. Weatherford (*Negro from Africa to America*, p. 249) reports certain instances in which Negroes were discriminated against in favor of whites, first, by assigning to white workers the better paying types of piece work, and second by assigning them more permanent jobs.

The most conclusive single instance of the inequality of pay between white and Negro workers comes from the teaching profession. Negro school teachers in the South, doing a given kind of work, are almost uniformly paid lower wages than white teachers who do similar work.

Teachers in Maryland elementary schools, holding third grade certificates, with 4 to 5 years experience, are paid $650 per year if white, and $360 per year if colored. Holders of first grade certificates, with 9 or more years experience receive, as maximum salary: if white, $1,150; if colored, $680. Differences in the salaries of high school teachers are equally great. (*Report of the Maryland Inter-Racial Commission,* 1927, pp. 7-8.)

The following instances of salary discrimination are cited by T. J. Woofter, Jr. (*Negro Problems in Cities,* pp. 205-6): The schedule of salaries in Lexington, Kentucky, provides for a minimum of $1,000 for white elementary teachers and a maximum of $900 for colored elementary teachers. The minimum for white high school teachers in Lexington is $1,400, while the maximum for colored high school teachers is $1,200. White teachers receive $35 additional pay for summer school work, and Negro teachers, $20. The annual increase to white teachers is $50; to Negro teachers, $25. In Memphis, Tennessee, the minimum salary for white elementary teachers is $1,000; the maximum is $1,600. The minimum for colored elementary teachers holding certificates is $720, and the maximum is $1,020. Similar discrimination appears in the high school salaries. The minimum salary for white elementary teachers in New Orleans is $1,200; for colored elementary teachers, $1,000. There are similar discriminations in the New Orleans high schools. The minimum salary for any white teacher in the public schools in Norfolk, Virginia, is $1,000. $1,000 is the maximum salary for any Negro elementary teacher in the same city. (*Opportunity*, February, 1926, p. 49.) Similar discriminations between teachers' salaries appear throughout the South.

Teachers' salaries are usually fixed by law. In many southern cities and states the laws discriminate arbitrarily against Negroes. "Whatever may be the Negro's training, efficiency or acquired ability, no matter how long he remains in the system, his economic status ends where that of the white teacher's begins." (J. O. Thomas, "Economic Deadlines in the South," *Opportunity*, February, 1926, p. 49.)

Negro teachers may have done as much or more preparatory work. They may hold certificates and diplomas from identical institutions. They must pass certain qualifying tests. They may have a record as good as that of white teachers. Even where they have a better record, they receive less wages for their teaching.

Negroes who enter the industries or the professions in competition with whites frequently receive less pay for equal work. A Negro must have higher recommendations and greater abilities than a white man requires to obtain and hold the same job. As one Negro worker put it, "We must have qualifications plus, and it is up to some white man to determine what that 'plus' means."

Where Negroes and white workers begin at the same wage level, in similar occupations, they soon find themselves far apart. The pay of the white workers advances, while the pay of the Negroes stands still. The white workers are promoted. The Negro workers stay at the bottom of the ladder.

On the other hand, Negroes get wage cuts before the whites. Most of the Negroes are unorganized. Many of them are unskilled. They have little power of mass protest. Their places can be easily filled by workers, Negro and white, who are anxious to take the jobs. Consequently the white employers, faced with the necessity of reducing overhead and cutting down expenses, begin with the Negro. During the late winter and spring of 1928, when wage cuts were being generally put into effect throughout the United States, the Negroes in Northern cities were almost invariably the first sufferers.

"They have started their wage-cuts with us," one Negro worker in Pittsburgh said. "Our wages have been cut thirty percent in the last four months. The Negro worker has no rights the white boss is bound to respect."

Some Negro workers are paid the same wages as white workers who do the same jobs. Other Negro workers receive less pay for the same work. The wages of white workers are advanced more rapidly than those of Negroes, and the wages of Negroes are cut before the wages of whites. When it comes to promotion, however, there is no comparison between the opportunity before the two races.

Occasionally Negroes are promoted to the position of foremen over other Negroes: Rarely do they act as foremen over white workers. In almost all cases where Negroes work, they work under white foremen. Here, however, the promotion opportunity of the Negro ends. Managers, superintendents, directors and executives of corporations controlled by white stockholders are almost invariably white. There may be unnoted exceptions, but they are so rare as to be for all practical purposes non-existent. The administration and executive direction of American industrial activity is in white hands. Negro enterprises employ Negro executives. But Negro enterprises cover less than 1 percent of the field of American industrial enterprise. Management in American industry is a white man's function in which Negroes have no opportunity to participate.

Negroes find employment at unskilled and semi-skilled occupations. Within the last ten years they have been able to penetrate the field of skilled occupations to a limited extent. Occasionally they succeed in getting white-collar jobs. In rare instances they occupy posts as straw bosses and foremen. Managerial positions in American industrial undertakings are closed to members of the black race.

Promotion, beyond the lowest rungs of the industrial ladder, is almost out of the question as far as Negroes are concerned. This holds true without any reference to the ability or training of the individual Negro.

Negro labor is replaced by white labor at the moment hard times begin. As a Negro employment manager stated the case, "Our people are the last to be hired and the first to be fired." In support of his contention he cited several instances in which Negro workers had been taken on during boom times and dismissed as soon as the boom had subsided.

In some cases Negroes who had worked for years with a perfectly clean record were dismissed before white workers who had been employed a comparatively short time.

Frequently it is difficult to prove that the Negro has been dismissed because he was a Negro. The employer gives no reason except that he no longer needs his man. In the spring of 1928 six colored elevator operators were working in a Chicago office building. One Friday night at 6 o'clock they were handed their pay and told that they need not come back. One of these men had been employed at the same job for 26 years; a second had worked for 16 years, a third had worked for 22 years. All six were given the finest recommendations, but the next day when the building opened, white operators were on the elevators.

The same thing holds true for the building trades. Where Negroes are allowed to work, employers usually take care of the white workers first. "Many people feel that the Negro has no right to a job while a white man is walking the street unemployed," said one Negro who had been faced with the loss of his job and the impossibility of finding another in the same trade during a temporary industrial depression. At this difficult time when the number of unemployed exceeded five millions, Negroes were not only dismissed at the same time as whites, but Negroes were dismissed and immediately replaced by whites.

Economic inferiority is constantly emphasized in the experience of the American Negro worker. Usually he cannot get the same job as the white man. When he gets the job, in many instances he does not receive the same pay. Even if he is paid at the same rate he has less of a chance of promotion and a greater chance for dismissal than the white man or woman on the same job.

Negro wage workers have learned these facts through bitter experience. They carry the normal burden of workers under capitalism. In addition they must shoulder the special burden of economic discrimination which the exploiting whites of the United States have laid upon the shoulders of Negro workers in industry.

13: NEGRO CENTERS IN INDUSTRIAL CITIES

NEGROES migrate to industrial cities, struggle against great obstacles to secure jobs and find themselves discriminated against on the job. They face another problem equally difficult—the problem of a living place.

Where can Negroes live in industrial cities?

Southern plantation Negroes and farmers had their own cabins, their own districts, in some cases even their own towns. They were largely self-sufficient economically.

When they enter an industrial city the Negroes find themselves in a new and hostile environment. Many of the Northern industrial cities, before 1910, had practically no Negro population. Where there was a Negro population, as in Philadelphia or Chicago, it was confined to well recognized living quarters.

The migration created a new situation. Industrial centers that had few Negroes were called upon to accommodate thousands. Tens of thousands of Negroes flocked into Chicago, Detroit, Pittsburgh, New York, Philadelphia. These Negroes had two chief objectives: a job and a living place. They got the job in competition with white workers. They found the living place by driving whites out of their homes.

Most American whites refuse to live in the same neighborhood with Negroes. Many whites, when Negroes attempt to enter a new neighborhood, either start legal action, resort to mob violence, or move away. Thus the Negroes who entered industrial centers found themselves face to face with a racial hostility which met them not only on the economic field but with equal intensity on the social field.

The Negro migration was unusually rapid. It came

at a time when building costs were rising and when building activities were slowing down. An army of Negroes demanded city living accommodations at the same time that an army of whites was moving from the country to the city.

Whites in many of the principal industrial centers were in a panic. They wanted to keep their homes. They refused to live in the same neighborhood with Negroes. The Negroes, pressed by the growing demand for housing accomodations, forced their way farther and farther into white neighborhoods.

Living opportunities for Negroes differ in different industrial cities. In Philadelphia, for example, which has an unusually large Negro population, Negroes have acted as servants for many generations. As the city grew, the houses of the masters were built on the main street and on the back streets and alleys were the houses of the servants. Originally, therefore, Negro quarters were built wherever the houses of well-to-do whites were constructed.

Such a system of housing Negroes corresponded, however, to the pre-industrial period. It could accommodate only the Negro house servant. The Negro laborer and the Negro machine hand must find some other solution for the housing problem. As the migration of 1915-1916 increased, the problem of Negro housing in industrial centers became constantly more acute.

"Where do Negroes live in New Haven?" I asked one of the leading representatives of the race in that city.

"We go where we can get a rent," answered my informant. "It is not every place that they will take us. The Jews and Italians will generally rent to us. Others will not."

"But do none of the Negroes here own their houses?"

"Indeed, we do. It is the only way that we have to

be sure of a place to live, but when we go to buy and the real estate man finds out that we are Negroes the price is always $2,000 or $3,000 higher so that we must struggle hard to meet it."

"When colored people move into a block, the whites move out," said a Negro real estate man in Washington, D. C. "I am living on a very nice residence street. When I moved in there were two or three colored families on our side of the street, and none on the other side. Now there is not a white family in the block. As soon as one colored family moves into a neighborhood the houses on both sides are vacated by the whites and remain vacant until some colored families buy them or rent them."

The National Association for the Advancement of Colored People reported: "The greatest issue faced by the Association during 1915 was that of residential segregation. This discriminatory practice arose in three forms: attempts at residential segregation through property-holders' covenants; efforts toward that end through mob violence; legislation designed to force Negroes to live in restricted areas." (*Crisis*, March, 1926, p. 229.)

Property-holders' convenants were contracts entered into by the residents of a certain block or district, under which they agreed not to sell or rent to Negroes for a specified number of years. They were used, but with little effect, in Washington and other cities.

Segregation ordinances, adopted, ordinarily, by city councils, prohibited Negroes from living in white neighborhoods and prohibited whites from living in Negro neighborhoods. The first segregation ordinance was passed by Baltimore in 1910. Then "a wave of residential segregation laws swept the country. City after city in the Southern and border states passed ordinances, the purpose and effect of which were to keep colored people from invading the areas which had hitherto been restricted to white residents. . . . More than a dozen cities, among them Baltimore, Maryland; Dallas, Texas; Asheville, North Carolina; Richmond, Virginia; St. Louis, Missouri; and Louisville, Kentucky; within a year passed such ordinances." (Arthur B. Spingarn, in an introduction to a pamphlet issued in 1926 by the National Association for the Advancement of Colored People, and dealing with the Louisville Segregation Case.)

There were four types of segregation laws: "(1) The ordinances passed by Baltimore apply only to all-white and all-Negro blocks, making it against the law for a Negro to move into a white block and vice versa. (2) The type passed by Virginia enables the cities to divide into segregated districts. This makes it unlawful for a Negro to move into a white district. (3) The type passed by Richmond, before the Statewide segregation act, legislates for the whole city, declaring that a block is "white" whenever a majority of the residents are white and "colored" when a majority of the residents are Negroes. According to this law a Negro can move into a mixed block when a majority of those residing in that block are Negroes. (4) Norfolk goes a step farther and determines the color of the block not only by the occupancy of the property, but also according to the ownership of the property within the block. In all of the ordinances, an exception is made in regard to domestic servants residing with their employers." (Duncan, *Changing Race Relationships*, p. 27.)

State courts generally upheld the constitutionality of these ordinances. The Lousiville ordinance was taken to the Supreme Court of the United States and was declared unconstitutional in a sweeping and unanimous decision.

The title to the Louisville ordinance read: "An ordinance to prevent conflict and ill-feeling between the white and colored races in the City of Louisville and to preserve the public peace and promote the general welfare by making reasonable provisions requiring, as far as practicable, the use of separate blocks for residences, places of abode, and places of assembly by white and colored people respectively."

The Sweet Case, in Detroit, arose out of the actions of a white mob that was seeking to prevent a Negro from occupying a house that he had purchased in a white neighborhood. Dr. Ossian W. Sweet, a young Negro physician, bought a home on Garland Avenue, Detroit, in May, 1925. Because of threats of violence, Dr. Sweet did not move into the house until September 8. That evening a mob gathered, but made no demonstration. The next evening, however, a larger mob collected and stoned the house. Shots were fired; one member of the mob was killed and one was wounded.

The police then arrested eleven occupants of the house and they were held for first degree murder. The case was tried in November. The Jury disagreed. (*Crisis*, January, 1926, pp. 125 ff. Report of the trial by Walter White.)

While Jews and Italians are generally more tolerant of Negro neighbors than other white persons, and while Jewish merchants frequently carry on retail businesses in Negro quarters, as a general rule, when Negroes have moved into a block of houses white people stop living there. One Negro real estate man said: "Except for business purposes white people never move into Negro districts. The Jewish merchants who come stay only until they get rich."

Residentially there are three classes of Negroes: roomers, renters and buyers.

The Negro roomer is either the floater who wanders from town to town and from job to job or else the newly arrived migrant from the South who has left his family and come North looking for work and perhaps ultimately for a place to settle.

Shortage of houses in which Negroes may live aggravates the problem of lodgers. Negro lodgers or roomers cannot locate in white families. They must find places with people of their own color. They cannot go to the same hotels with whites. They must find a hotel that is run for the accommodation of Negroes. In cities where the number of Negro homes is very limited, the pressure on boarding and lodging accomodations is necessarily very great.

A report on *Negro Housing in Philadelphia* (Philadelphia Housing Association, 1927, p. 17), calls attention to the fact that crowding is much greater among Negroes who rent than among Negro home owners. "In the rented dwellings the population is more than one per room. Much of this room crowding is due to previous habits of the migrants and much is due to high rents, while some of it is due to the necessity of the family to fit into any kind of dwelling that can be found."

Housing shortage and high rents are both responsible for the prevalence of roomers among the Negro city dwellers. Since it is difficult to find rooms and since rooms are very expensive, Negro families make what plans they can to rent or buy. Ordinarily they include in their budget an item of income from lodgers in order to assist them in buying or renting or in making payments on their houses. The Philadelphia Housing Report notes that "only relatively well-to-do families are without lodgers."

Where large numbers of Negroes are employed at construction work or in other less permanent occupations they are usually housed in the most casual fashion. Thus the Bethelehem Steel Corporation at Sparrow's Point, Maryland, has two extensive stockades wired off from the rest of the town in which single Negro men can find lodgings. Within the stockade are rows of small wooden shacks, heated by stoves, containing four beds per shack. Negro workers who come there from the South are assigned to these stockades. They sleep in the shacks, eat in a common dining-room and have their washing done in a common laundry. The company supplies a number of Negro janitors whose duty it is to clean the shacks, the eating room, the wash rooms and grounds.

The whole appearance of these stockades is unbelievably desolate. They contain no opportunities for social life. The lodgers who occupy the beds sleep, eat and attend to their personal needs. Such living quarters represent the lowest level of lodgings for the migratory worker.

The renting negro meets many obstacles. First, he is limited in the neighborhoods to which he can go. In general it is only the older houses which are rented. New houses are primarily built for sale. This is particularly true in the case of the Negro. Even real estate operators who build to rent will not rent to Negroes if they can rent to whites, since one Negro family in a neighborhood practically means the elimination of the whites from that territory. Negro renters must therefore content themselves with the oldest and least desirable city properties. In those run-down neighborhoods which are gradually being transformed from white living quarters to Negro living quarters the coming of the Negroes means an immediate increase in rentals. This may seem strange, but it is a phenomenon which is commonly reported from all of the cities where there has been a large Negro migration.

As living quarters become less and less desirable, whites are willing to pay less and less rent, landlords make less and less repairs and property deteriorates.

Negroes enter the neighborhood. Whites leave. Buildings stand temporarily empty, but as the Negro tenant comes in with his unusually large number of dwellers per room, the real estate man raises rents to correspond with the paying capacity of their new tenants.

Negroes are undesirable tenants, therefore they must pay. Negroes have many boarders and lodgers per family, therefore they can afford to pay. The report on *Negro Housing in Philadelphia* shows a weekly rent per dwelling in the Negro neighborhoods of $7.95. "Certainly considering the scanty equipment and the poor repair of the average Negro dwelling, $7.95 is comparatively high." (P. 22.)

This report comes from a district in West Philadelphia which has just been converted into a Negro district.

A representative of the Urban League in Buffalo, New York, said, "Negroes pay 33 1/3 to 50 percent more rent than whites pay for the same accommodations." There is less segregation of Negroes in Buffalo than in any other Northern industrial city.

Leila Houghteling (*Income and Standards of Living of Unskilled Laborers in Chicago*, p. 112) notes that "more than 80 percent of the colored families spend 20 percent or more of the earnings of the chief wage earner for rent, while among white families only 30 percent paid that large proportion." The table on page 113 of the Houghteling study shows that 5 percent of the white families and 44 percent of the Negro families spend more than 30 percent of the earnings of the chief wage earner for rent.

Negroes buy homes where that is at all possible. The Negro house owner is no longer at the mercy of real estate operators. He has a home which he can pay for on the installment plan, with the aid of his wife's earnings and the income from boarders and lodgers.

Negro home buyers have transformed the position of the Philadelphia Negro. While the Negro continued to rent he was compelled to live where the real estate men would permit him. Since he has become a buyer he is to a greater degree his own master. Negro neighborhoods have sprung up in the North Philadelphia and West Philadelphia in a territory that was formerly under the exclusive control of the whites.

The census of 1920 gave the following facts about Philadelphia Negroes:

Number of families	30,995
Living in Rented Houses	26,984
Living in Owned Homes	3,778
Homes Free of Debt	724
Homes Mortgaged	2,479

The progress of Negro home ownership in Philadelphia has been greatly facilitated by the development of Negro building and loan associations. In 1910 Pennsylvania had 8 colored building and loan associations, with a total capital of $150,000. In 1924 there were in Philadelphia 34 associations with a total capital of more than $5,000,000. One of these is 25 years old and has financed the purchase of homes for Negroes to an amount in excess of $1,000,000. (*Negro Housing in Philadelphia*, p. 28.)

Negroes buying homes must ordinarily pay higher prices than whites for the same accommodations. Frequently they assume third mortgages, borrowing money at ruinous rates. Still, in the industrial centers in the past 15 years they have been able to extend their home ownership rapidly and widely. It is the home-owning Negro who succeeds most effectively in breaking through the Negro pale.

Negroes in industrial centers usually live in Negro

settlements or Negro pales. Until the war when migration was relatively small, these Negro pales were definite in extent. With the rapid growth of the Negro population and the increase in Negro home ownership, these Negro pales extended in area and multiplied in number. T. J. Woofter, Jr. (*Negro Problems in Cities*, p. 40 ff) prints a series of maps showing the Negro settlements in the most important cities of the United States. In almost every case they represent a high percentage of concentration.

The Chicago Commission on Race Relations made a study of housing in one of the principal Chicago industries employing Negroes. The white workers in the industry were scattered throughout Chicago and its suburbs. The Negro workers were largely concentrated in one small area on Chicago's south side—the chief Negro area of Chicago. (*The Negro In Chicago*, p. 107.)

Woofter notes that the Negro pales or settlements in various industrial centers differ with the size of the center and the character of the city. In New York and Chicago, for example, the concentration of Negroes is very great but in a relatively small portion of the city area. "In New York 96 percent of the white people are concentrated in white areas and 28 percent of the colored people are in concentrated colored areas." (*Negro Problems in Cities*, p. 38.)

A second group of cities, which includes most of the larger southern cities, has Negroes concentrated in several rather large parts of the city "and lightly scattered in others, thus leaving a large proportion of the white people in areas from 10 to 90 percent Negro. In Richmond, 53 percent of the white people are in concentrated white areas and 25 percent of the Negroes in concentrated Negro areas." (*Idem.*)

The older Southern states show another situation.

The proportion of Negroes in the total population is high. The Negroes live generally throughout the city. "In Charleston, there are no enumeration districts that have a population of less than 10 percent colored and none that have a population of less than 10 percent white, placing all members of both races in districts from 10 to 90 percent colored. (*Idem.*)

Woofter includes a fourth group of cities with small Negro populations in which the Negroes are widely scattered. These instances, however, are relatively unimportant in the total problem.

Summing up the general situation of the Negro segregation in industrial centers, Woofter writes, "While segregation is practically never complete, all cities have some areas where the large majority of the population is Negro. It is in these areas that the masses of the Negroes live." (*Ibid.*, p. 39.) It is also worthy of note that in those northern cities to which Negroes have recently migrated in large numbers and in which therefore the race problem is most acute, exclusive Negro areas are very large and segregation is very complete.

Population density in Negro areas of industrial centers is very much greater than population density of white areas in the same cities. In some instances the density is four times as great in the Negro sections as in the white sections. In New York, where the Negro density is greatest, it is 336 per acre. (*Ibid.*, p. 78.)

Thus the Negroes in industrial cities live in concentrated population areas of relatively great density, paying high rents, purchasing houses at high prices and struggling constantly to extend the area in which they may live in order to accomodate the influx of migrating Negroes. Woofter notes that these Negro colonies in industrial cities have certain traits in common: "They are large, the largest Negro neighborhood usually being centrally located. The South side, in Chicago, probably

the largest Negro community in the world, numbers
126,000 people. Harlem, in New York, though not a
typical central section, numbers 124,000; the South
side in Philadelphia, 51,000; Central Memphis, 22,000;
and Central Atlanta, 18,000. These are such great
aggregations of population that each has a community
life all its own. They contain the large churches,
schools, theatres, centers of commercial recreation and
business houses. The main arteries, Lenox Avenue in
Harlem, State Street in Chicago, South Street in Philadelphia, Beale Street in Memphis, Second Street in Richmond and Auburn Avenue in Atlanta are business
streets of bustle and activity, and are the main
thoroughfares for thousands of people. The central
position of these sections also subjects them all to invasion by business and manufacturing establishments
and to the subsequent depreciation of property for residence purposes." (Woofter, *Negro Problems in Cities*,
p. 100.)

Negroes in American industrial cities are not legally
segregated. The Supreme Court decision in the Louisville case forbade that. But they live by themselves.
Each important industrial center has its Negro quarter,
separated from the surrounding white living quarters.
Whites do not move into Negro living quarters unless
they wish to carry on business there. Negroes who attempt to enter white quarters find themselves face to
face with serious economic and social obstacles.

Where can the Negro who is seeking for industrial
employment find a home? If he is a boarder or lodger
he is almost compelled to go among his own people. If
he wishes to rent or buy, manifold restrictions hold
him within the Negro pale. The result is that in the industrial centers to which Negroes have recently migrated the masses of Negroes live in restricted areas
which are subject to constant inundation by fresh bands

of migrants from the seemingly inexhaustible supplies of migrant labor from the South.

How does the Negro live in industrial centers?

In the first place, the housing accommodations which the Negro roomer or renter is compelled to accept are of necessity poor. The buildings which he occupies are in the oldest part of town, therefore they are usually unprovided with modern sanitary and other conveniences. Then the extreme overcrowding of Negro neighborhoods renders the housing situation doubly difficult.

Negroes are for the most part unskilled or semiskilled, low paid workers, unable to pay high rents or to buy their own homes. They cannot pick and choose but must take what offers at the prices that are within the range of their incomes. The result is that the Negro quarters are not only in the older parts of town but are overcrowded and poverty-stricken to an extreme degree. The well-to-do Negroes who are able to buy expensive homes escape some of the worst of these evils of congestion and overcrowding. The Negro masses, however, are constantly subject to them.

Visit any typical industrial city and inquire for the Negro quarter. Sometimes it is along the railroad, as in New Haven, Connecticut. In other places it is along the banks of some dirty stream, as in Akron, Ohio. Again it is in some abandoned section which is being gradually converted from residence into business property, as in South Philadelphia. Occasionally, to be sure, a whole great city area, as South Chicago or Harlem, is occupied by the Negro. Such cases are exceptional, however. The Hill District in Pittsburgh and the East Side in Cincinnati are typical instances of conditions to which Negroes are subject when they move from their plantation homes in the South in search of higher wages and shorter hours in some industrial oasis of the North.

Akron citizens reply to your question, "Yes, the Negro quarter is under the viaduct."

You cross the business center of town, pass down a street that leads to a lower level and find yourself beside a polluted stream. Here are coal pockets, lumber yards, railroads, mud roads. Ashes and refuse are dumped along the stream banks or lie in piles in the open lots. Small wooden shacks, shanties and houses scattered along the banks of the stream, within easy reach of flood water, provide the homes in which the lower paid Negroes of Akron live. The place is unsightly, unhealthy. Probably it is the least desirable residential section of Akron. It has nothing to commend it to the migrant Negro except low rents, the presence of other Negroes and the fact that it is easier to get along in this Negro community than it is to try to find a place in more desirable surroundings.

Or climb the hill above the Union Station in Pittsburgh. The streets are ill-kept, dirty. The houses are dilapidated. Some of them are even abandoned. Many of them are built of wood. Throngs of unemployed Negro workers stand gossiping at the principal corners. The whole community bespeaks poverty, neglect and physical hardship.

Perhaps Negro housing conditions in industrial areas are at their worst on Chicago's South Side. Scores of thousands of Negroes—workers, business people, professional people—carry on the routine of life under circumstances which would seem to be impossible in a modern community. Many of the alleys and small streets are unpaved, covered with litter, garbage, offal.

Enter this alley in the center of Chicago's South Side. Passing vehicles have gouged deep ruts in the oozing black muck. Your foot slips. You are ankle deep in the slime. You secure a better foothold and push forward. The stench from a dead, decaying dog greets you. Ashes and tin cans are piled in over-flowing boxes and barrels. A huckster wagon sloshes along through the mire.

Through the broken, patched wooden fences and the half-open gates of back yards you glimpse the rubbish. Three Negro women stand gossiping at one back gate. They stare, with ill-concealed hostility. Why a white man here? An inspection, perhaps! Behind a neighboring gate a savage dog leaps and barks. Some wooden shanties used as living quarters, front on this noisome alley. Two children prowl through the refuse.

During rainy periods and particularly in the spring and fall it is practically impossible to approach these houses without wading through inches of mud. Rubbish is piled in the yards as it is piled in the street. Houses are being used which have long since been unfit for habitation. The whole neighborhood reflects the pressing necessity which compels human beings in the second largest city of the United States to accept living quarters which under no possible stretch of the imagination can be considered decent.

The Chicago Commission on Race Relations reported the result of a thorough-going investigation of Negro housing as follows:

"On the South Side, where most of the Negro population lives, the low quality of housing is widespread, although there are some houses of a better grade which are greatly in demand.

"The ordinary conveniences, considered necessities by the average white citizen, are often lacking. Bathrooms are often missing. Gas lighting is common and electric lighting a rarity. Heating is commonly done by wood or coal stoves, and furnaces are rather exceptional; when furnaces are present, they are sometimes out of commission.

"Under the heading of 'Housing Conditions' such notations as these are often found:

"No gas, bath or toilet. Plumbing very bad; toilet leaks; bowl broken; leak in kitchen sink; water stands in kitchen; leak in bath makes ceiling soggy and wet all the time. Plastering off in front room. General appearance very bad inside and out.

"This is the common situation of the dweller in the districts mentioned." (*Negro in Chicago*, pp. 152-3.)

All Negroes do not live in such squalor. The housing standard of the well-to-do Negro is equal to that of the well-to-do white man. But the masses of Negro workers take the broken victuals of American housing facilities.

Negro housing in Philadelphia, Baltimore, Washington and other cities on the borderline between North and South presents one of the most acute problems which these communities must face. In Washington, within sight of the capitol, there are hundreds of wooden shacks and shanties in which Negroes are crowded together under conditions of slum living that would shame any twentieth century municipality. Housing conditions surrounding the life of the Baltimore Negro are only slightly better than those which exist in Washington.

Harlem offers housing accomodations which are superior to those in some of the similar Negro communities in industrial centers, although congestion is more severe in New York than in any other Negro center of the United States.

Harlem is unique in many respects. All types of Negroes mingle there. Every imaginable type of activity is carried on in this black city within a white metropolis.

James Weldon Johnson calls Harlem "the greatest Negro city in the world," with "more Negroes to the square mile than any other spot on earth." (Locke, *The New Negro*, p. 301.)

When Negro mothers and fathers move to industrial areas their children grow to adulthood surrounded by physical and social conditions of a very low order. Instead of securing from society the best that life has to give, these Negro children literally receive life's worst. They lack sunshine, fresh air, sanitation and cleanliness, play space, normal recreation. They are outcasts, living in the least desirable parts of town; in the poorest houses, subject to the most intense exploitation. From infancy these children feel the pressure of subjection.

Negroes in industrial centers suffer from an adverse environment. As a matter of course they are the victims of insufficient income.

Houghteling's study of *Income and Standards of Living of Unskilled Laborers in Chicago* (p. 187) gives a number of typical illustrations of family conditions in the homes of unskilled laborers. One colored family, for example, "consists of father, mother and three children—a boy of 13 and girls of 12 and 10 years. This family of 5, with 3 men roomers (one also a boarder) lives in 5 rooms. The house is equipped with a bathroom, one stove, a furnace and gas plate. Five double beds are used by the group. The house is shabbily furnished and is very much overcrowded. The mother does day work and the boy of 13 peddles on the street after school hours. Their earnings, together with those of the father, made the total yearly family fund $2,052."

Negro mothers are very generally workers. Houghteling writes: "A far greater proportion of the mothers in the Negro families worked than in the white families. From a total of 87 Negro families, 41 mothers or 47.1

percent worked in comparison with 67 white mothers, 17.8 percent of the 377 white families reported on." (Pp. 56-7.) The author notes, however, that this may be due to the "lower wages paid the colored men and the need for supplementing income."

Negroes are usually unskilled or semi-skilled workers. In these capacities, they command the lowest incomes. Low income means bad housing, inadequate food, and the other curses that go with poverty.

The Negroes in industrial centers are crowded into segregated pales because they are Negroes. Their low income forces the mother to join the father as a wage-earner outside of the home, and makes adequate care of the children of Negro industrial workers difficult or impossible.

Low incomes, congested living, bad housing are reflected in the excessive sickness and death rates among the American Negroes. Frederick L. Hoffman of the Prudential Life Insurance Company and Louis I. Dublin of the Metropolitan Life Insurance Company have both devoted considerable attention to the question of Negro health. Dr. Dublin writes, in the North "we find the mortality among Negroes invariably higher than among whites." (Dublin, *Health and Wealth*, p. 259.)

"The colored death rate of Baltimore is ranging from 60 to 70 percent higher than the white rate." (Baltimore Urban League, *Study of the Death Rate of the Baltimore Negro*, p. 1.) The white death rate in Baltimore for 1925 was 12.84 per thousand of population. The colored death rate for the same year was 24.88 per thousand. The five year average showed a death rate for whites of 12.9 per thousand and a death rate for Negroes of 22.5 per thousand. (*Ibid.*, p. 2.)

Death rates in Baltimore for children under one year for 1924 were 74.4 per thousand for whites; 125 per thousand for Negroes. In 1925, 68.1 per thousand for

whites; 118.9 per thousand for Negroes. (*Ibid.*, p. 12.)
The Baltimore survey adds, "This excessive death rate of
colored persons as compared to white is not confined to
Baltimore, but exists in approximately the same degree
in other places. In support of this contention, the Baltimore Urban League study (p. 19) cites infant death
rates per thousand as follows:

City	White	Colored
Kansas City	80	172
Norfolk, Va.	53	144
Louisville, Ky.	66	178
Indianapolis	69	136
Washington	64	134

Certain diseases such as tuberculosis are widely prevalent among Negroes in industrial centers. The Negro
death rate from tuberculosis in Baltimore in 1925 was
358 per one hundred thousand; the white death rate
was 83. In this case the Negro death rate was more
than four times the white death rate in the same city
for the same disease. (*Death Rate of the Baltimore
Negro*, p. 27.)

Chicago's pulmonary tuberculosis death rate per
hundred thousand in 1925 was, whites, 58; Negroes,
366. In this case the Negro death rate for pulmonary
tuberculosis was 6 times the white death rate.

Difference in the death rates between Negroes and
whites are less extreme in some of the smaller cities.
In Trenton, New Jersey, for example, an Urban League
survey made in 1925 shows the white death rate to
range from 10 to 13 per thousand of population. For
the same period the colored death rate ranged from 16
to 18 per thousand of population.

Sickness and death rates give an excellent idea of the
adverse conditions which Negroes are forced to face
in some of the principal industrial centers to which they

have migrated so freely during the past fifteen years. The Negro men and women, born and brought up in the Southern countryside, and Negro children born in the South and reared in the North, alike find difficulty in adjusting themselves to congestion, insanitation, lack of sunshine and fresh air which go with the housing quarters inside the Negro pales. The result of this lack of adjustment shows itself in the unusually high death rates among Negroes as compared with death rates among whites in the same community.

Home buying by Negroes has done more than any other single factor to overcome the obstacles faced by Negroes in industrial areas. The Negro roomer or lodger was forced to content himself with quarters inside the Negro pale; the Negro buyer can break through the pale at the edges and by extending his purchase to other sections of the city set up new quarters in which the living conditions surrounding the lives of the Negro are vastly better than those in the older, more congested and more restricted Negro housing areas.

Negroes have not found their place in industrial America. They are still a subject race. They must content themselves with the left-overs in their occupations and in their living quarters. Except in those comparatively few instances where a Negro family can afford to buy itself into better physical surroundings, the children of most Negro unskilled and semi-skilled workers are forced to grow up under circumstances which threaten the health, the well-being and even the life itself to a degree that is practically undreamed of by the great majority of white children growing up in the same industrial centers.

14 : ECONOMIC PENALTIES OF BLACKNESS

UNDER the best of circumstances the American Negro looking for an industrial job pays the price for his color. In the first place, he is limited in the range of occupations among which he may choose. In the second place, he is limited within each occupation to the less desirable positions. Third, his income and opportunity for promotion on the job are below those of the white workers.

Job owners, in the United States, are white men. Negro ownership is largely confined to farms, homes and personal belongings. The business activities in which they are engaged are generally restricted to small scale merchandising.

Where are the majority of American workers employed?

A third work in manufacturing and mechanical industries.

A sixth are employed in agriculture.

The other three-sixths are working for wages or salaries in transportation, in clerical occupations, in mining, in certain professional occupations (chiefly school teaching), or else they are engaged in trade.

The manufacturing and mechanical industries are "white" industries. First because they are found chiefly in the North where the population is overwhelmingly white; second because, until very recently, these industries were only slightly developed in the South, where the majority of Negroes lived; third, because until the War of 1914-1918, the Northern industrialists employed but few Negroes and those in unskilled and menial capacities. Negroes have never held jobs in many manufacturing and mechanical industries. As for owning or directing them—such a thing is almost unheard of in the North and is rare in the South. The control of one-third of all the jobs in the United States—the manufacturing and mechanical jobs—is a virtual white monopoly.

Negroes operate 925,708 farms out of a total of 6,558,000 in the United States. Among the Negro farmers the percentage of farm tenancy is 76.2 percent. This would mean that the actual number of Negro farm owners does not exceed a quarter of a million.

Furthermore, as compared with farms owned by the whites, the Negro farms are relatively small. Take Virginia as an example. The average acreage for white farms in Virginia is 117.7 acres. The average acreage for Negro farms is 47.5 acres. Thus the Negro farms are only two-fifths the size of white farms. (Brown, *Educational and Economic Development of the Negro in Virginia*, University of Virginia Publications No. 6, p. 92.)

The Negro owned and operated farms are, for the most part, in the cotton belt. They are handled not by hired labor but by the working farmer and his family. The big truck, grain, stock, dairy and fruit farms—the farms which hire the bulk of farm labor—are in the North, North Central and Western parts of the United States, where the Negro population is the smallest. The great majority of these large farms are owned and worked by whites. The hired labor on them is, in most cases, white.

Railroads, street railways, electric power stations, telephone and telegraph, radio and other public utilities are a virtual white monopoly, which Negroes have scarcely touched. This holds true both as to ownership and as to management, although it is doubtless more true of management than it is of ownership. Negroes may (and occasionally they do) own railroad stocks and bonds. They never sit on boards of directors, nor do they occupy the higher administrative positions which are responsible for the shaping of policy.

Mining and lumbering—two of the important and basic industries in any modern industrial society—are owned and directed, in the United States, by white men.

Whites fill most clerical positions in the offices of banks, insurance companies, industrial and transport corporations. Even where Negroes are occasionally employed, direction remains in the hands of the whites.

These are the chief job openings in the United States —including at least four-fifths of all the wage and salaried workers. With the exception of farming, they are managed and directed by whites. Thus the right to hire and fire in the United States is a white man's function. The Negro asks a white man for an opportunity to work. The white man tells the Negro when he no longer needs his services.

Within the last few years there has been some development of Negro business. Negro storekeepers, Negro contractors, Negro professional men and women, Negro insurance companies, Negro banks, Negro fraternal societies and Negro improvement associations make a practice of hiring Negro workers. The total number of Negro professional and business men is small, however. The businesses directed by them are generally very limited in size. Few of them have any direct relation to the basic industries. The total volume of Negro business is negligible compared with that of the white business world. In any basic industry except farming, Negro ownership is probably restricted to less than 1 percent of the total for the United States.

There are, to be sure, Negro stock and bond owners who participate in the ownership of business and who as stockholders are theoretically responsible for its management. Practically, however, the leading American industrial and public utility enterprises are owned by whites. Even where Negroes are stockholders they are minority stockholders. The ownership of American industrial capital remains largely in the hands of the American whites and the management is almost exclusively white.

Probably 99 percent of all jobs in the United States that are secured by Negroes, other than farm jobs, are secured from white employers, white managers, white foremen and from corporations whose stocks and bonds are controlled by members of the white owning class.

To be black, in the United States, is to be proletarian. A larger proportion of Negroes are "gainfully employed" than is to be found in any other United States racial grouping. Among native whites, 46.6 percent are gainfully employed (1920 Occupations Census); among whites with foreign or mixed parents, 49.7 percent; among Negroes, 10 years of age and over, 59.9 percent (three-fifths) are gainfully employed.

Among Negro males, 81.1 percent are gainfully employed, as compared with 75 percent among native white males.

Among Negro females, 38.9 percent are gainfully employed, as compared with 17.2 percent for native born white females of native parents and 24.8 percent for native born females of foreign or mixed parents.

Among Negro children 10 to 13 years of age, 19.5 percent of the boys and 13.1 percent of the girls are gainfully employed as compared with 5.5 percent of native white boys of native parents and 0.9 percent of the girls; 1.2 percent of the native white boys of mixed parentage and 0.4 percent of the girls.

Job ownership in the United States is a function of the white race. Negroes are job takers from white job owners. Until twenty years ago this division, except in Southern agriculture, was almost complete. The owning class was a white class. The Negroes made up a working class. Recent modifications, particularly since the world war, have changed to a slight degree the truth of this generalization. Nevertheless the main control of industry still rests in the hands of the whites. Ownership is theirs very largely; domination is theirs completely.

Before the Civil war, slave holding in the Southern states was a white man's function. Exceptional Negroes held slaves. The overwhelming majority of slaves, however, were owned by the whites, worked for whites, produced economic surplus upon which whites could live.

United States industry (job ownership) is today a white man's country. White men make up its citizenship almost exclusively. Whites are the stock and bond and mortgage holders—the executives, managers and directors.

There are a few Negroes among the job owners and managers. But they are almost never admitted to full citizenship. In enterprises controlled by white men they are seldom promoted to the more responsible positions. They are not accepted in business associations and clubs on a basis of equality with the whites. Even though Negroes may become rich, they cannot become job directors in the real sense of that term.

Black men who enter this white man's country of American job ownership enter as inferiors. They are job takers. The white man is the owner; the boss to whom the black man must say: "Can I have a job? Where must I work? What must I do?"

The whites are the exploiters; the blacks are the exploited. The line between the two is a color line. Where the blacks participate as stock and bond holders in the general system of exploitation, they do so to only a very slight degree. When blacks go to white men asking for jobs, they go in competition with whites asking for jobs.

The white job owners give the white job-takers first choice. The black job-takers get the leavings.

Economically, American Negroes must constantly pay the penalty of their blackness. They are exploited as a race. No matter what their individual abilities, professional or technical training, their success or achievements, their position in the field of economic endeavor is always less favorable than that of whites having the same qualifications.

Negroes are the victims of economic discrimination directed against blacks because they are black. This discrimination was practiced before the Civil War when Negroes were slaves; it is practiced today when Negroes are "free." It is a part of the technique employed by exploiting whites to keep exploited blacks in a position where they can neither resist nor escape exploitation.

2. *Negro boy in front of Negro home in South Chicago.*

1. *Negro backyard in South Chicago.*

*3. Negro children making mud pies in South Chicago
street.*

4. Where Negro children live and play in South Chicago.

5. *Alley in Negro quarter of South Chicago.*

6. *Negro homes in South Chicago.*

7. Negro children, Hill District, Pittsburgh.

8. Negro tenements, Hill District, Pittsburgh.

9. Negro child in Pittsburgh's Hill District.

10. Negro housing, Hill District, Pittsburgh.

11. Pittsburgh. Unemployed Negroes. Winter of 1928.

12. Under the viaduct, where the Negroes of Akron, Ohio, live.

14. Negro street in Philadelphia.

13. Backyard in South Philadelphia.

15. Negro bootblack, Philadelphia.

16. Two of Baltimore's Negro children.

18. Negro children in Detroit must get accustomed to low standards of food, housing, clothing.

17. Negro children, Baltimore.

19. Negro merchant, Detroit.

20. Housing, Detroit Negro quarter.

22. *A Negro couple in Harlem, New York City.*

21. *Negro housing, Washington.*

23. *Barracks provided by Bethlehem Steel Company for Negro workers, Sparrows Point, Md.*

24. *800 Negro men live in these barracks, 4 men per room, Sparrows Point, Md.*

26. *Negro children playing in the streets of Harlem, New York City.*

25. *Unemployed Negroes, Philadelphia.*

27. *Brownstone fronts, Harlem, New York City, occupied by Negroes.*

28. *Rear of brownstone fronts, Harlem, New York City.*

30. *Negro postman in Harlem, New York City.*

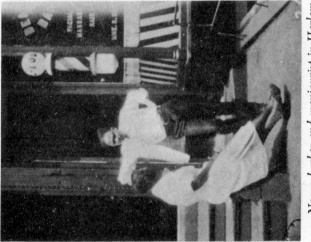

29. *Negro barber and manicurist in Harlem, New York City.*

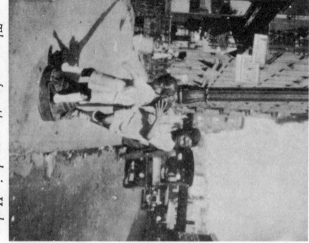

31. *There are few playgrounds in Harlem. Negro children must play on the streets.*

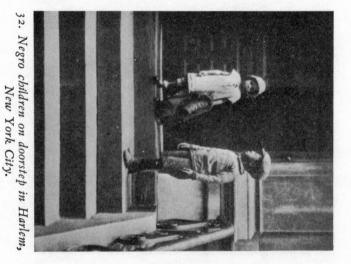

32. *Negro children on doorstep in Harlem, New York City.*

15 : THE COLOR LINE

MANY Europeans find it difficult to understand the "color line" in the United States. Living in countries where all of the people are of the same general race stock they cannot realize the intensity with which race lines are drawn when two obviously different races mingle over a very large territory.

Color lines are sharp in the United States. The twelve million Negroes who make up a tenth of the total population are separated from the whites and in most respects are forced to keep to themselves. This is true in the North and West, where Negroes make up a very small percentage of the total population. It is doubly true in the South where Negroes are always a large proportion and sometimes a majority of the population. In the South, race lines are inexorable.

What is the "color line" in the United States?

People who are not white are "colored." This colored class includes—besides the Negroes—Indians, Chinese, Japanese, Hindus, Malayans. The fundamental human division in the United States, is made on the most obvious of characteristics: skin color.

Negroes, for the purposes of the United States census, are usually divided into "blacks" and "mulattoes." The term "black," as employed in the census of 1890, denoted: all persons "having three-fourths or more black blood." Other persons, having any least proportion of Negro blood, were classed as "mulattoes."

This is the accepted approach to the American color line.

A person does not become "white" by having white blood in his veins. On the contrary, the presence of Negro blood in his veins keeps him "colored."

State laws differ.

Persons descended from Negroes to the third generation inclusive, though one ancestor in each generation may have been white, are colored in Kentucky, Maryland, Mississippi, North Carolina, Tennessee and Texas.

Negro blood in the ancestry at any point within five generations makes a person "colored" in Alabama.

Those who have less than one-fourth Negro blood are not "colored" in three Northern states: Michigan, Nebraska, Oregon. But one-eighth Negro blood makes a person "colored" in Florida, Georgia, Indiana, Missouri and South Carolina.

A visible and distinct admixture of African blood makes a person colored in Arkansas and Virginia.

Oklahoma, in its Constitution, carries the color line to the limit: "Whenever in the Constitution and laws of this state the word or words 'colored' or 'colored race' or 'Negro' or 'Negro race' are used, the same shall be construed to mean . . . all persons of African descent."

Thus the Southern States, and most of the border states lying between the South and the North have fixed the color line by law. On one side of this line men are white—and superior. On the other side they are colored—and inferior.

That is the next, logical step. First people are separated according to skin color. Then, those with colored skins are classed as racially inferior.

The belief in white racial superiority is one of the most deep-seated and generally accepted of all the ideas held by the people of the United States. Americans take white racial superiority for granted and act accordingly whenever they encounter members of any colored race.

Racial inferiority as interpreted by the people of the United States carries with it fearful penalties:

1. Members of the inferior races are the hewers of wood and drawers of water. They are deliberately denied opportunities for economic advancement, and, so far as possible, they are required to do the heavy, dirty work of the country.
2. Socially they are outcasts.
3. The children of inferior (colored) races grow up branded and cursed with their inferiority. Their parents are paid the lowest wages; the children live in the worst slums; go to the poorest schools; come into contact with the least desirable social environment; have the fewest cultural opportunities; suffer most acutely from poverty, disease, neglect.

All alien peoples have paid this penalty to a certain degree in the United States. This has been true even of Irish, Germans, Scandinavians, whose customs and language were their chief distinguishing characteristics. Slavs, Italians, Greeks, Mexicans have felt the pressure more severely. Racial lines have been still more sharply drawn against Chinese and Japanese. But the deepest race lines are those which separate the Negroes from the whites: because the two races are so obviously different; because the Negroes were slaves; because they are so numerous; because the marks of race difference persist, in one generation after another.

Irish, Germans and Scandinavians were quickly absorbed into the white American population. After one or two generations they disappeared as a distinct racial or nationalistic group.

Slavs, Italians, Greeks and Mexicans followed the same course, though more slowly. They too were "white," and therefore "superior" Americans.

The Orientals, never very numerous except on the West Coast, remained aloof, and were treated as alien, inferior people.

Negroes, with their obvious racial characteristics, after more than three centuries on American soil, are still treated, in every way, as inferior. The penalties attached to that inferiority are more severe, and they are more diligently enforced by the whites against the Negroes than in the case of any other racial group in the United States.

The color line is drawn against the American Negro in every sphere of life.

1. It is drawn in all those relationships which bring people together socially; which might normally be expected to result in friendships; which make possible more or less intimate contacts between the sexes. In school fraternities; in fraternal orders; in clubs; in the Y. M. C. A.; in churches; in church organizations; in social gatherings; in outings; on excursions; at summer camps and recreation centers, Negroes do not and cannot mingle with whites. In almost all of these institutions Negroes are to be found: shoveling coal; wiping up the floors; cleaning the toilets; cooking; waiting on the table; washing dishes; running errands. As menials they are met with generally; as social equals, almost never.

2. Negroes cannot meet whites, in the United States, on a basis of equality in the more intimate social relations. Consciousness of their racial "inferiority" is forced upon them in most public institutions. Theatres, movie houses, amusement and recreation centers, hotels, restaurants, soda-fountain, stores, commonly discriminate against Negro patrons. They employ Negroes in inferior and menial positions. They refuse to accept them on a basis of equality with white patrons. This is generally true in the South. It is almost equally true

in those Northern cities with large Negro populations. It is less true in Northern centers where the
Negro population is small.

3. Negroes are publicly segregated: in certain housing areas; in certain districts; in Negro waiting
rooms; in special compartments of street cars and
in "Jim-Crow" cars on railroad trains; in schools;
in hospitals; in Y. M. C. A.'s; in churches. This
is generally true in the South. It is true to a less
extent in those sections of the North which have
large Negro populations.

4. When Negroes violate law or convention, lynching parties shoot them, hang them, burn them.
This is particularly true in the South. Race wars,
that is, mass white attacks on Negroes, have occurred all over the United States. The most spec-
tacular race war in recent years took place in
Chicago, a city with a population of 2,600,000
whites and 109,000 negroes (census of 1920).

5. Underlying the entire area of race discrimination
is the persistent and practically universal position
of economic inferiority forced by the whites upon
the Negroes. During the slave period Negroes
did field work, house work, acted as body servants
and did many kinds of skilled craft work. They
were carpenters, bricklayers, masons, plasterers,
blacksmiths, machinists, textile workers. Since
slave days many Negroes have been trained in
trade schools. But they cannot get work at skilled
occupations. The discrimination against them is
practically universal, extending into all of the
principal skilled occupations for which wage-
workers are hired. Where Negroes are employed
in the major industries, they usually do unskilled,
menial work. And in many instances they receive less pay than whites for the same work. This

is notoriously true in the case of public school teachers in the South, where the salaries of Negro teachers are far below those of white teachers with identical training. Negroes have little difficulty in finding jobs as unskilled laborers, janitors, roustabouts, field hands. The moment they enter the semi-skilled or skilled trades they are restricted in every direction. This is probably more true in the North than it is in the South. Throughout industrial United States Negroes are consistently discriminated against because they are Negroes. This economic discrimination, which determines income, is, of course, the most drastic of all, because it holds the Negro in a position where he and the members of his family are permanently denied an opportunity to raise their cultural standards.

Every Negro in the United States—every member of the race, irrespective of his qualities or his talents—because he is black, is swept ruthlessly into the category of "racial inferiority" and held there with all of the power of the superior, exploiting, white race. Negroes in the United States are exploited and suppressed because they are Negroes. They are on the wrong side of the color line. Socially and economically they are forced to pay the penalty of belonging to a subject race.

16: RACE SUPERIORITY

THE color line is a line separating the "superior" white race from an "inferior" black race. The white race has drawn the line. The white race adopts the measures necessary to guarantee that the members of the black race shall not cross it.

Negroes, as members of an "inferior" race, must be kept in their place.

What is their place?

Inferiority: at the bottom of the economic and social ladder.

How can Negroes be kept there?

By establishing and maintaining clearly marked lines between the races; by keeping the races apart; by preventing race mixture, or anything leading in that direction. The superior race must assert itself and maintain its superiority at all costs and on every occasion.

The problem of keeping Negroes in their place as members of an inferior race varies directly with the number and the proportion of Negroes in the total population. Where the number of Negroes in a town or city is negligible, there is practically no race problem. Where, on the other hand, Negroes predominate or form a large portion of the population, the problem is acute. Southern States have been the scene of most race conflict in the past because it was in the South that most Negroes lived. Recent migrations of Negroes to the North, with the corresponding increases of Negro population, has made the problem of keeping Negroes in their place a most important social issue in many border and Northern states.

The distribution of race friction and race conflict can be roughly gauged from the distribution of Negro population. Negroes make up less than 1 percent of the population in Western United States. In the industrial states they constitute from 1 to 3 percent of the population. In the South, they are more than one-fourth of the total population. In ten Southern States, the Negro population is more than a quarter of the total population. In two states it is more than half.

These were the states in which the race problem assumed its most extreme form. The South generally—that is, the territory in which slavery persisted down to the period of the Civil War and in which the Negroes still live and do the heavy work, particularly in agriculture—maintains a comparatively unified position on the race problem. In the South the Negroes constitute an inferior race, and the Southern whites spare no pains to emphasize the fact.

Particularly in the South a relentless struggle has been and is being waged to prevent the assimilation and amalgamation of the American Negroes with the American whites. This struggle is basic in the whole problem of keeping Negroes in their place.

Elaborate restrictions are maintained covering all social relations between the races. Since Negroes are inferior they must not mingle with the whites on any plane of social intimacy or equality. This principle is enforced in the South; it is adhered to more or less rigidly throughout the whole of the United States.

Negroes are ordinarily excluded from social gatherings. Where they are present they come on sufferance and are usually made to feel their separateness. This holds particularly true at the top of the social scale. It is less emphatic among the working masses. In radical and revolutionary circles it is virtually non-existent.

Negroes do not participate in more or less formal social relationships, such as those involved in outings, excursions, summer camps, recreation centers, receptions.

If a Negro is included in such a social function even in the North the case is sufficiently exceptional to attract notice. Social institutions in which friendships are built up and in which social relations of a more permanent character are maintained almost always exclude Negroes.

Contacts between the sexes are the subject of peculiarly stringent restrictions.

Such formal relations between the sexes as walking along the street, sitting in the parks, attending the movie or the theatre are not only frowned upon, but they may easily become the subject of mob action.

A young white woman and a very black Negro recently walked together along 86th Street, New York City. The whole street turned to stare.

New York is one of the freest places in the United States in so far as race relations are concerned, yet, so rarely do members of the opposite sexes of the two races appear together on the streets that such a couple attracts almost universal attention.

In less cosmopolitan cities, a black man walking on the street with a white woman may be insulted, jeered, stoned. Police rescued such a couple from a mob of hoodlums in one of the largest cities of the United States. Their lives had been actually endangered.

Public opinion in smaller centers refuses to tolerate any such relationship. Black men and white women must not associate publicly. Those who attempt to do so suffer grievous consequences.

Blacks and whites may not dance together in public. A radical organization in New York City arranged a public dance at which black men danced with white women. Because of this the police stopped the dance.

New York radicals gave a dinner-dance in a well-patronized Chinese restaurant. Negro men danced with white women. A guest, from another part of the restaurant, attempted, by force, to stop the dancing.

◆ 157 ◆

If such stringent restrictions upon the relations of blacks and whites are imposed in New York City, it is easy to imagine the rigor with which public relations between the sexes are restricted in other cities and in smaller communities.

The two races must not mix. Even formal public relations between the sexes is practically taboo.

As for marriage between the races, it is prohibited alike by custom and by law.

The announcement, in a northern city, that a white girl is about to marry a colored man brings front page publicity in the newspapers. It may also lead to mob violence.

Marriages between the races in the South are both illegal and unconstitutional.

Six Southern states—Alabama, Florida, North Carolina, South Carolina, Mississippi and Tennessee—have adopted constitutions which include provisions against intermarriage. The constitution of Alabama, for example, adopted September 3, 1901, Article 3, Section 102 reads: "The legislature shall never pass any law to authorize or legalize intermarriage between any white person and a Negro or a descendant of a Negro."

Delaware, Maryland, Virginia, West Virginia, South Carolina, Georgia, Florida, Alabama, Louisiana, Kentucky, Tennessee, Arkansas, Oklahoma and Texas, together with the Northern states of Colorado, Indiana, Idaho, Nebraska, North and South Dakota, have adopted laws under which the marriage of whites and Negroes is prohibited. In Arizona, California, Mississippi, Missouri, Montana, Utah and Oregon, marriage of whites with Orientals is also prohibited. North Carolina prohibits the marriage of whites with Negro and Crotoan Indian blood, and Nevada with persons of the Ethiopian, Malay, Mongolian or American Indian races. (*Negro Year Book*, 1925-6, p. 241.)

Twenty-nine states have laws on their statute books prohibiting intermarriage between whites and Negroes.

The *Negro Year Book* states the situation in this way: "The general rule with reference to intermarriage between races is this: 'If the applicant for a marriage license had even only one great-grandparent who was a full-blooded Negro he may not receive a license; but if that great-grandparent were a mulatto and in all later generations mating took place (illegally, of course) with a white person, then the person in question is legally white and may marry a white person. Otherwise stated, the descendant of a Negro to the third generation inclusive, though one ancestor in each generation were pure white, is excluded; or persons having one-eighth or more of Negro blood are excluded from marrying a white person. In Nebraska and Virginia, the limit is set at one-fourth or more of Negro blood. The State of Georgia sets no limit, but declares 'marriage between white persons and persons of African descent is forever prohibited; such marriages are null and void.' Louisiana forbids the marriage of whites to 'persons of color'." (Pp. 241-2.)

Savage legal penalties are imposed, particularly in the Southern States, for the violation of these provisions against intermarriage. In some cases these penalties include ten years in the penitentiary.

There is a strong movement to extend the prohibition on intermarriage. The National Association for the Advancement of Colored People, in its annual report for 1927, cites six states—Connecticut, Maine, Massachusetts, Michigan, New Jersey, Rhode Island—in which anti-intermarriage bills were introduced into the legislatures in 1927. None of the bills was passed. It is significant that all of these states were in the North and that four of them were in New England.

Marrying between whites and blacks is illegal and unconstitutional in the South. Mating is frequently visited with fearful penalties. Cases of lynching are on record where the sole charge against the Negro man was that he had had sex relations with a white woman. The question of her consent was not an issue. The *Crisis* of November, 1922, page 37, published the following letter from Florida:

> "It might be interesting to know that on the night of the 14th of July, Jake Davis of Colquit, Georgia, was lynched, charged with being the father of a child by a white woman. It appears that the woman gave birth to a Negro child and her neighbors insisted that she tell the father of the child, which she did with the usual result. The interesting fact is that the State press took no notice of it. It was not in the papers."

In this instance a black man was punished for mating with a white woman. In the reverse situation where a white man mates with a black woman, the Southern mob frequently takes its vengeance on the black woman.

Since all race crossings are beyond the pale, the offspring of race unions tend to be social outcasts. They are neither black nor white. Consequently they suffer the disadvantage of social ostracism from both races.

Despite the legal discouragement and the various penalties imposed by mob law on mating between whites and blacks, particularly in the South, the amount of race crossing is considerable, as shown in the number of mulattoes.

Maryland forbade intermarriage by a law of 1663. (Reuter, *Mulatto in the United States*, pp. 129-132.) A century later (1775) a census returned 8 percent of the Maryland Negroes as mulattoes. At that time Maryland had one-sixth of the Negro population of the country. (*Ibid.*, p. 112.)

United States Census figures show an increase in the number of mulattoes during recent years. In 1850 there were 405,751 mulattoes for the entire United States. Twenty years later (1870) the number was 584,049; in 1890, 1,332,060, and the figure for 1910 was 2,050,606. The Census of 1920, taken under slightly different conditions from those prevailing in 1910, reported only 1,660,554 mulattoes. Even at that, however, the number for 1920 would be three times as great as the number for 1870 and four times as great as the number for 1850.

Recently a very careful study was made of race crossing in the cases of 1,551 American Negroes. The results showed a wide admixture of non-Negro blood. "Instead of 80 or 85 percent of the American Negroes being wholly African in descent only a little over 20 percent are unmixed, while almost 80 percent show mixture with white or American Indian or with both stocks. (Herskovitz, *American Negro*, p. 10.)

Furthermore, and this is the significant item in the Herskovitz study, the race crossings are producing a type that is biologically new. "In trait after trait, if one measures them and computes their variabilities, and if one then compares these with the variability in the same traits of unmixed African, European or American Indian populations, one will find that in most of the traits measured the variability of the greatly mixed American Negroes I have measured is as low as, or lower than, that of unmixed populations from which it has been derived. (*Ibid.*, pp. 21-2.) This might have been foreseen since: "There is in his ancestry all of the principal racial elements of which humanity is composed—white, Negro and Mongoloid. And from this mixture there is being welded, and is already discernible, a definite physical type which may be called the American Negro." (*Ibid.*, p. 19.)

The white "superior" race in the United States makes every effort to keep at a social distance from the black "inferior" race, and it spares no pains to prevent the admixture of black with white blood. Nevertheless the crossing of races goes steadily forward—illegally, informally, secretly, but none the less effectively, resulting in a new type that is already discernible.

17: CONSCIOUSNESS OF BLACKNESS

NEGROES cannot mingle with whites in the United States on any plane that implies intimate personal relations. This is particularly true of relations between the sexes.

The principle is carried very much further, however. Consciousness of their racial inferiority is constantly forced upon the Negroes by a widespread system of discrimination and exclusion levied against them on no other ground than their skin color.

The term "discrimination" as here used means refusal to grant Negroes equal rights with whites. In its extreme form it leads to exclusion and segregation—forcing Negroes into separate organizations and groups.

Negroes are usually excluded from amusement and recreation centers managed and patronized by whites. Of course this is true in the South. It is becoming noticeable all over the North.

After an extended investigation, H. G. Duncan writes: "In parks the color line is also being drawn in the North. It is strange that it should be drawn here as parks are usually very spacious, and the races do not have to come very close together, but the Northern whites do not seem to desire to be near a Negro so they are drawing the line. Negroes are excluded from all of the popular parks in Cincinnati, and even from the Municipal Bath House. In Indianapolis they come in contact with the 'bungaloo gangs' who beat them frightfully and run them out of the parks. In Chicago the white people, with ropes and guns, rid Gage Park of Negroes. The fearful race riot in Chicago last July was started because the white people were trying to drive the Negroes from a bathing beach. . . . At Clemington,

New Jersey—the Atlantic City for the poor—Negroes are allowed to go there but one day in the year. On the day the Negroes are permitted to go all the white people stay away. In Boston the Negroes are practically excluded from many of the parks, playgrounds, baths, hospitals and museums." (Duncan, *Changing Race Relationships*, pp. 68-9.)

Theatres commonly discriminate against Negroes. On the borderline between the North and South, in Baltimore, for example, formerly Negroes sat anywhere in the balcony. Now they are placed in the last two rows of the balcony. Negroes have never sat downstairs in Baltimore theatres or movie houses. Within the past two years they have been compelled to take seats on the last two rows of the balcony, or to stand.

The same general practice prevails in New York. The Negro patron goes to the theatre for tickets: "The house is all sold out except . . ." says the ticket agent as he hands his Negro customer tickets for the special Negro section.

Perhaps the Negro has sent a white friend to buy tickets for the lower floor. The Negro presents these tickets at the door on the evening of the performance: "There is some mistake," the doorkeeper says. "These tickets are not for tonight. But if you want seats for tonight"—in the Negro section.

Otherwise: "These seats are already taken. We are very sorry. Wait a moment, and I will fix you up"— with tickets for the Negro section.

Throughout the North discrimination against Negroes is practiced in amusement parks, theatres and other recreation centers. In Youngstown, Ohio, for example, Negroes are assigned to a segregated section in the theatres. Even in New Haven, Connecticut, which has a population of less than 8,000 Negroes, a Negro who has lived in the town for many years said, "I used to go to the Hyperion Theater once a week and sit anywhere I wanted. Now colored people are being placed in a special section of the theatre. Other seats are always sold out when we ask for them."

Hotels, restaurants and eating houses quite commonly discriminate against Negroes. Negroes in the South take it for granted that they shall go to hotels and restaurants run for Negroes. In the North, however, such establishments are fewer, and the Negro frequently finds it hard to get accommodations.

Northern hotels and restaurants carry the principle of discrimination so far that in many instances dark-skinned men from India have been refused hotel accommodations on the assumption that they were Negroes.

The New York *Nation* (February 8, 1928) printed the following communication:

"A student at Lincoln University, who was with me last summer in Russia, stopped in Philadelphia on his way back from a speaking engagement. Having a few hours for a chat, we picked the Russian Inn.

"We placed our coats on the rack near the entrance. The hostess arose from her chair and eyed me with utter amazement. Her eyes said: 'Now you, above all people, should have more sense than to do this. Shame on you!' But she said nothing. Instead she tapped the proprietor, who was sitting at a table with some friends, on the shoulder. He arose and said to us: 'Do you want to use the telephone?'

" 'Yes. And please reserve a table for us.'

" 'I'm sorry, but we can't do that.'

" 'Why?'

" 'Just so.'

"My friend was amused and took it philosophically.

" 'I wasn't treated this way in Russia,' he said.

"As we left the place he smiled. 'Sol,' he said, 'I see you know nothing about your own country.'

"My friend is a Negro."

The instance is typical. In 1928, the New York *Nation* gave a series of dinners to celebrate the anniversary of Oswald Garrison Villard's connection with the paper. One of these dinners was announced for Baltimore, and was to be held in a leading hotel. A Negro subscriber to the paper sent a check to the Chairman of the Dinner Committee and requested a reservation. The Hotel refused to serve the dinner if a Negro attended and Mr. Villard refused to attend the dinner unless Negroes were welcome. After searching Baltimore for a hotel or restaurant in which the dinner could be held, it was finally given in the private residence of one of the committee members.

Another Baltimore hotel refused to permit a Negro speaker to address a meeting of a luncheon club composed entirely of whites, unless he put on the uniform of a bell-boy. The hotel manager explained: "No Negroes other than servants ever go above the first floor of this hotel."

New York hotels, which are among the most cosmopolitan in America, follow the same general rule. In March, 1928, a New York writer was stopping at one of the leading hotels on lower Fifth Avenue. A Negro friend came to see the writer on three different occasions. On the fourth occasion he was told to take the service elevator in the rear of the hotel. "Negroes do not ride in the elevator with our guests," the elevator operator explained.

The writer protested to the hotel manager. The manager responded genially, "Theoretically, of course, you are right, but you know that I am conducting a hotel on lower Fifth Avenue, and you know that Negroes do not ride in passenger elevators of Fifth Avenue Hotels. I must make my choice. If I want to run a hotel here, I must ask Negroes to ride in the back elevators."

Restaurants are compelled, under the law in most states, to serve any guests who apply. If Negroes are refused directly, the matter may be taken into the courts. Generally, therefore, the restaurants do not refuse service. They simply let the Negro guests wait for an hour or two before the order is taken, and then for another hour or two before the food is served. "In many restaurants the waiters put a spoonful of pepper into the milk and a spoonful of salt into the coffee sold to a Negro; or charge him five times the regular price for a sandwich, and give him a glass of dishwater to drink. I know of no first class restaurant in any Northern city that will serve Negroes." (Duncan, *Changing Race Relationships*, p. 63.)

Stores and shops frequently request Negroes to trade in the basement or in sections of the store designated for Negroes, or they make their objection to Negro customers so evident that the Negroes fail to come back. One Negro woman in Baltimore said that she could buy buttons and similar commodities in one of the leading Baltimore department stores, and she was always very courteously treated, but that she was not allowed to try on shoes, hats, dresses or gloves. In another store if she wished to buy a hat she could try it on provided she went into a special room designated for the purpose.

Another Negro described a visit to a candy store on a main street in Washington: "When I went into the store, every person from the manager to the last salesgirl turned and stared at me. Nothing was said, but they continued to stare while I made my purchase and hurried out of the store. They let me have the candy that I wanted, but I was made to realize that colored people do not go into that store to buy candy, and I never went again."

H. G. Duncan writes: "Race prejudice has developed so in the North that many of the best men's furnishing stores, ladies' furnishing stores, shoe stores, etc., will not serve Negroes. I have observed in several towns and cities in the North that in the best stores where the wealthy white people trade, Negroes are not served under any consideration, even at extortionate prices." But, the writer adds: "I do not know a case of such discrimination in the South." (Duncan, *Changing Race Relationships*, pp. 63-4.)

In educational and health institutions, conditions vary widely. In northern New Jersey, for example, Negroes attend the same schools with whites and enjoy the same facilities. In southern New Jersey, on the other hand, Negroes attend special schools and are subject to sharp discrimination.

The most drastic educational discrimination, however, is met with in the South. Schools for Negroes receive smaller appropriations; teachers are less well paid; funds for maintenance are smaller; special features and equipment are seldom provided for Negro schools. Only a very small percentage of southern cities have libraries to which Negroes can go. In Mississippi there are 49 special agricultural schools for whites. There are no such schools for Negroes.

During the spring of 1928 a meeting of the Workers International Relief was held in the Labor Lyceum on Miller Street, Pittsburgh. The district adjoins the leading colored residence section of Pittsburgh. A number of Negroes attended the meeting and sat together in the main part of the auditorium. But during the same month in Washington, D. C., a meeting held in Typographical Hall, under the same auspices, was attended by fourteen Negroes. All fourteen sat together on one row at the extreme rear of the hall. They made no attempt whatever to mingle with the white persons in the audience. They accepted their exclusion from the body of the meeting as a matter of course.

A special study by Helen M. Street, *Hospital and Dispensary Care of the Colored in Baltimore*, shows that while the sickness and death rates were very much higher for colored than for whites, the amount of hospital space allowed to the colored was considerably less in proportion than that allowed to the whites.

Many newspapers, particularly in the South, never print "Miss," "Mrs." or "Mr." before the names of Negroes who are mentioned in their columns. A leading Baltimore Negro recently made a detailed study, extending over several months, of the *Baltimore Sun*. All news matter and all editorial comment that was in any way related to Negroes was clipped and filed. In more than 400 clippings the names of Negroes were always printed as "Sadie Brown," "John Jones," etc. A study of the clippings also made it quite evident that whenever a Negro was guilty of a crime the fact that he was a Negro was consistently played up throughout the news story.

A Northern Negro travelling in Mississippi went into a post office to ask for stamps. In answering the postmistress he failed to say "Yes, Ma'am." He was sharply reprimanded by a man in the post office and when he returned to the Negro home in which he was being entertained and related the story, he was urged to leave town at once for fear that he might suffer some bodily injury.

Another Northern Negro walked into a Southern store and asked for a can of Prince Albert smoking tobacco. The storekeeper demanded, "What did you ask for?"

"Prince Albert," replied the customer.

"Nigger," said the store-keeper, "look at that package," pointing to the picture of Prince Albert on the outside of the tobacco container. "What did you want?"

"Mr. Prince Albert," replied the Negro. He got his tobacco and the incident closed. In the South no Negro is permitted to refer to a white man except by the title of Mr.

Discrimination against Negroes because of their race is general in the South. It is frequent and growing in the North. Before the recent migrations, in some of the far northern cities it was practically non-existent. In big centers like Chicago, Detroit, Pittsburgh, where there has been a large influx of Negro migrants, discrimination is becoming more and more pronounced.

No Negro can escape this discrimination unless he happens to be so light that he is not recognized as a Negro. In all of his contacts with the world of white folks the consciousness of his blackness is insistently forced upon him.

DISCRIMINATION against the American Negro, in its extreme form, appears as public exclusion or segregation. According to this segregation principle, Negroes are compelled to spend their time with other Negroes, except when they are working for the whites.

Segregation in the South is very complete. In the border cities and states the idea is widely accepted.

Negroes generally live among Negroes. This fact is so widely accepted, even in the North, that a Negro neighborhood is one in which whites neither rent nor buy, while the advent of a Negro renter or buyer is a sign for the whites to leave the neighoborhood in which the Negro appears.

Whites have enforced Negro housing segregation by law, by contract, by gentlemen's agreements, by brute force.

Legal segregation and segregation by covenant were sufficiently discussed in the opening pages of Chapter XIII, "Negro Centers in Industrial Cities." At the present time segregation is being effected by gentlemen's agreement and by brute force.

Effective segregation results are achieved by a general agreement among real estate men. This agreement is adhered to except in the twilight zones between colored and white neighborhoods. There, in the industrial centers, the waves of Negro migration are persistently beating down the obstacles which the white owning class has tried to set up against Negro invasion of white residence territory.

Where laws and covenants fail, mobs sometimes succeed. Negroes are not permitted by whites to live in certain parts of the United States. This is true, for example, in Waverly, Ohio. "A Negro is not permitted to stay over night under any consideration in Syracuse, Ohio. Some months ago 'night-riders' appeared and drove all the Negroes out of New Madrid, Missouri. There are certain counties in Indiana and Illinois that do not permit a Negro to dwell within their boundaries. Lawrenceburg, Ellwood and Salem, Indiana, have not permitted Negroes to dwell there for years." (Duncan, *Changing Race Relationships*, p. 33.) The *Negro Year Book* for 1925-6, page 385, lists 68 towns and 23 settlements inhabited exclusively by Negroes.

These are extreme cases, comparatively few in number. Negro housing segregation, though, however enforced, is general. In the larger cities, there are recognized Negro quarters in which whites seldom live and to which Negroes are more or less effectively confined. In smaller industrial centers, in villages, and even in the open country, Negro segregation persists.

Negroes must not only live by themselves in most parts of the United States, but in many sections they must travel by themselves. Laws for the separation of Negro and white in public conveyances are in force in Tennessee, Florida, Mississippi, Texas, Louisiana, Alabama, Kentucky, Arkansas, Georgia, South Carolina, North Carolina, Virginia, Maryland and Oklahoma. (*Opportunity*, February, 1924, p. 43.) Such separate conveyances for Negroes are commonly known as "Jim Crow" cars.

The first "Jim Crow" cars were run in Massachusetts in 1841. Immediately after the Civil War the idea of the "Jim Crow" car invaded the South. Florida and Mississippi passed laws in 1865, providing that no freeman, Negro or colored, may ride in a first-class passenger car set aside for white persons, except "in the case of Negroes or Mulattoes, travelling with their masters in the capacity of nurses." This latter clause quoted from the Laws of Mississippi (1865, p. 232), tells the story of the position of the Negro as effectively as may be. Negroes accompany whites anywhere provided they go in an inferior capacity. Maryland has a segregation law, passed in 1904, under which passengers travelling within the state must be separated along race lines. Georgia passed a law in 1891 that provided for the segregation of the Negroes in street cars. Louisiana passed a similar law in 1902; Mississippi in 1904; Tennessee and Florida in 1905; Virginia, 1906; North Carolina and Oklahoma in 1907. Where separation in street cars is not provided for by state law, Southern cities pass ordinances to achieve the same result. (Duncan, *Changing Race Relations*, p. 61.)

Negroes cannot get Pullman berths south of Washington, D. C. If a Negro secures Pullman accommodations by sending a white man to buy his ticket, word is telegraphed along the line ahead of the train, a mob gathers and the man is pulled off. On May 1, 1928, one of the leading Negroes of New York travelled from Memphis to New York by Pullman. He bought a drawing room, kept the shades drawn and the door closed, and by good fortune succeeded in escaping detection. He was ill at the time and felt that the game was worth the candle.

Under a law passed in Virginia in 1926, white and colored persons are forbidden to sit on the same floor. The law was aimed at a particular institution, but it indicates the extent to which the white ruling class of the South is willing to go in segregating the Negro population.

The insurance business affords another example of exclusion. Until 1912 there were no Negro insurance companies doing a general business, and with the exception of the Metropolitan Insurance Company, none of the important American insurance companies would write policies for Negroes. The Metropolitan, the largest insurance company in the United States, has a special department for handling Negro business, with about 2,000,000 policies in force on Negroes. Most of these are industrial policies. The second largest insurance company, the Prudential "for many years has insured no Negroes, even in its industrial department." (H. H. Pace, "Business and Insurance Among Negroes," *Crisis*, September, 1926, p. 220.)

In the summer of 1928 a prominent American Negro stated that he had recently made an attempt to secure insurance policies, and that the agents of a number of companies who had come into his office in response to his request told him very frankly that they did not care to write insurance on Negro risks, except for a very limited class of policies.

As lately as 1910 an insurance magazine stated that "the amount of life insurance carried upon the lives of Negroes is so small as to be almost negligible." After 1913 the insurance business among Negroes increased rapidly. There are now eight old line legal reserve life insurance companies, administered by Negroes and catering to Negroes exclusively. Three of these companies also do an industrial insurance business. (Pace, "Business and Insurance Among Negroes," *Crisis*, September, 1926, p. 219.)

Negroes attend Negro schools in many parts of the United States. Throughout the South, of course, Negroes are strictly segregated in their own educational institutions. In border cities like Baltimore, Indianapolis, St. Louis, segregation in the schools is almost as strict as it is in the South.

Separate school laws with respect to races are in force in Alabama, Louisiana, Delaware, Florida, Georgia, Kentucky, Arkansas, Maryland, Mississippi, Missouri, North Carolina, Oklahoma, South Carolina, Tennessee, Texas,

Virginia and West Virginia. (*Opportunity*, February, 1924, p. 43.) Massachusetts, New York, New Jersey, Ohio, Pennsylvania, Illinois and Nevada once had separate schools. It was in these states that the idea originated. Seven states prohibit separate schools. (Duncan, *Changing Race Relationships*, p. 35.)

Many cases are on record of segregation in schools where there is neither state nor municipal regulation. This is true in southern New Jersey and southern Pennsylvania. The same thing is true in Kansas, Indiana and Ohio. Eighteen Illinois counties maintain separate schools for Negroes. (*Ibid.*, pp. 37-38.)

So widely is the principle of segregation in educational institutions accepted, that Bulletin No. 39, *Statistics of State School Systems*, published in 1927 by the U. S. Bureau of Education, contains a number of tables in which a separation is made of students under columns headed, "white" and "colored."

Segregation in the case of educational institutions has also meant exclusion from educational opportunity. This is notably true in higher educational institutions.

Until recently, economic and social pressure made it practically impossible for Negroes to go to college. Between 1820 and 1870, only 66 Negroes graduated from American colleges. In 1820 there were 1,771,656 Negroes in the United States. In 1870, 4,880,000 Negroes. Between 1870 and 1900, 2,177 Negroes graduated from American colleges. In 1900 there were 8,833,994 Negroes in the United States. For all practical purposes, therefore, up to the beginning of the present century, American colleges were closed to American Negroes. This closing was readily made effective because there were practically no public high school facilities for Negroes, because preparatory schools generally refused to accept them, and because the ordinary Negro parents in receipt of scant incomes were in no position to provide higher education for their sons and daughters.

Negroes are excluded from the state universities in states like Missouri, as a matter of course. These state universities are maintained by public taxation. Negroes are citizens and taxpayers, yet their children are denied these publicly maintained educational facilities and they are offered no adequate substitute.

The barring of Negroes in higher educational institutions is still effective. "Out of the forty-four colleges in Pennsylvania, one of which is for Negroes, sixteen report never to have had a Negro student. Several others report to have had one, two or three, and those several years ago. . . . Discriminations against Negroes in colleges and universities seem to have increased very rapidly for the last few years." (Duncan, *Changing Race Relationships*, pp. 42 and 44.)

Twelve Negroes have attended West Point Military Academy—the first in 1870, the last in 1889. Three graduated.

Three Negroes have attended the Naval Academy at Annapolis, from 1872 to 1875. None ever graduated.

The situation is clear enough.

Reconstruction days gave Southern Negroes sufficient temporary power to enable them to elect members of their own race to the United States Congress. These Negro Congressmen enjoyed, among other privileges, that of nominating students to West Point and Annapolis. Hence the Negroes there. When the period of reconstruction ended Negroes ceased to sit as Representatives or Senators in Washington and neither from the South nor the North could their children secure the education necessary to give them officers' commissions in the Army and Navy of the United States.

The principle of race segregation is carried through the various social institutions of the United States.

Negroes have their own churches. The *Negro Year*

Book for 1925-6 (pp. 256 ff.) reports 47,000 Negro churches; 46,000 Negro Sunday schools; 5,000,000 Negro communicants; 3,000,000 Sunday School scholars, and church property valued at $98,500,000. The Year Book also includes a list of Negro denominations.

One of the active Negroes in Detroit, Michigan, was describing the position of the Detroit Negro colony.

"Are Negroes allowed to go to white churches in this city?" he was asked.

His reply was a classic:

"They can attend any church they want to, without being molested or insulted, provided they do not go in large numbers."

Other "Christian" institutions such as the Y. M. C. A. and the Y. W. C. A. accept and follow the principle of racial segregation.

The *Negro Year Book* for 1925-6, pages 278 ff., lists the Negro Y. M. C. A. and Y. W. C. A. organizations.

During 1927 one of the leading Negroes in New York City tried to get a son of seventeen into the Y. M. C. A. at Flushing, Long Island. The application was held up by the membership committee for more than five months, while the young man was being urged to join the "Y" in New York City, where there is a special organization for colored men. The boy was elected by his fellow students as the most popular student in the Flushing High School. He had an enviable record in every direction, except one—his color. That barred him from the "Y."

A leader among the Negroes in Buffalo, New York, described the maneuvering by which the Negroes of that city had been "persuaded" to organize a Negro Y. M. C. A. (paid for by subscriptions from white backers). "That is the entering wedge of race segregation in Buffalo," he said bitterly.

The Y. W. C. A. has 11 branches and centers in

Philadelphia—nine for whites and two for colored women and girls. The color line is rigidly drawn. Said one of the colored workers in the "Y":

> "No white girl would come into our pool, and no colored girl would be permitted to go into a pool in a white girl's Y. W. C. A."

The issue could hardly be more explicitly stated.

Fraternal orders generally segregate white and colored members. Elks, Odd Fellows, Masons and other fraternal societies maintain separate lodges for Negroes.

A prominent member of the American Bar Association vouched for the statement that no Negroes are members of the organization. One Negro got in after a struggle. The occurrence was never repeated. Proposers of new members are now asked the race of those whom they propose. The Bar Association has no rule on the subject. "It is just a practice," to use the words of the lawyer who was giving the information.

Negroes are ordinarily excluded from student fraternities. In Detroit City College the Negroes tried to meet the situation by organizing a fraternity of their own. Then they applied for admission to the inter-fraternity council. At last accounts their application had been awaiting action for more than a year. There are at least seven Greek-letter fraternities and sororities among Negro students in the United States.

Southern states, by law, segregate Negro workers. The National Urban League's survey of Baltimore reports that "Negroes and whites employed in the same establishments and engaged on the same process must be separately housed even if a mere partition accomplishes the segregation." Paul Blanshard reports a South Carolina cotton mill in which a mill superintendent was fined $110 for working employees over 60 hours a week and for allowing members of both races to work in the same room. (Blanshard, *Labor in Southern Cotton Mills*, pp. 68-9.)

The Standard Oil Company of New Jersey has a plant at Baton Rouge, Louisiana. Under the system of employee representation, the 1,500 Negro employees are specially represented by 12 Negro representatives. (*Opportunity*, April, 1923, p. 25.)

Many trade unions originally excluded Negroes from membership. The issue has been fought out during the past fifty years. At the present time a number of the international unions have removed the barriers to Negro membership. Many of them still segregate Negroes in special locals. This is particularly true in the South, where, however, comparatively little trade union organization has taken place among Negroes. Buffalo, New York, has a separate Negro Longshoremen's Union. There are a number of segregated Negro locals of the United Mine Workers of America.

The principle of segregation perpetuates itself consistently. "Segregation in the kindergarten stimulates a desire for segregation in the grades; when it is established in the grades, there is usually to be found a call for segregation in the high schools. Then the atmosphere within the universities becomes less tolerant toward any group which has already been cast out by the rest of the school system. Then, of course, people who are not fit to sit with you in college are certainly not good enough to sit with you in the moving picture shows, or on the street cars, or on the park benches. Segregation in the churches must logically anticipate segregation in Heaven. In New Orleans we have segregated grave yards—for segregation alive calls for segregation dead." (William Pickens, "Racial Segregation," *Opportunity*, December, 1927, p. 364.)

Jerome Dowd (*Negro in American Life*, p. 39)

reaches the conclusion that: "not only in respect to their place of residence, but in nearly every other respect, the Negroes in the North tend to live apart from the whites. The degree of segregation generally varies with the mass of the Negro population."

In a border city like St. Louis, Negroes are segregated in houses and apartments, in schools, playgrounds, hospitals, factories, churches, Y. M. C. A.'s and Y. W. C. A.'s, fraternal orders and practically all other social institutions and activities.

Negro segregation is practically universal in the South, widespread in the border states, frequent in the North. It is the extreme form of discrimination which affects the Negro in almost every contact that he has with the whites from one end of the United States to the other.

Negroes, as members of an inferior race, must be kept by themselves unless they are occupied in adding to the pleasure or profit of the superior white race. They are outcast socially as they are subjugated and exploited economically. The greatest virtue that an American Negro can possess is to know his place and stay in it.

*1. The schoolyard at recess. A public school for Negro
girls, Washington, D. C.*

*2. A segregated school for Negroes only, Washington,
D. C.*

3. Negro children in a South Chicago schoolyard.

4. Segregated hotel, for Negroes only, Florida.

6. Segregation in Detroit.

5. A Jim-Crow car for Negroes only, Fayetteville, N. C.

7. A Harlem "Back to Africa" announcement, Negro Club, New York City.

8. Negro segregation in Washington.

10. A segregated lunchroom, Richmond, Va.

9. Segregated toilets. One pair for white men and women, the other for Negro men and women. Atlantic Coast Line Railway, North Carolina.

11. Negro workers entering the side entrance, Atlantic Coast Line Railroad Shops, Florence, S.C.

12. Segregation section of a Virginia steamboat, Newport News, Va.

13. Only Negroes live on this Baltimore street.

14. Fifth Avenue, New York. Lower Fifth Avenue is exclusively white. In Harlem it is black—and not so exclusive.

15. Colored entrance, café, Birmingham, Alabama.

16. White entrance to same restaurant, Birmingham.

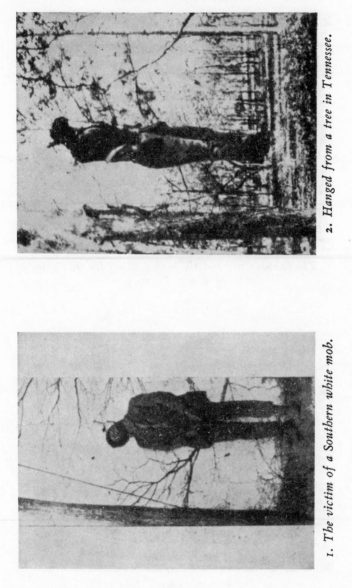

2. Hanged from a tree in Tennessee.

1. The victim of a Southern white mob.

3. The burning fire and the mob waiting for its victim in Waco, Texas.

4. The victim—burned to a crisp!

*5. The mob enjoys the gruesome spectacle to the end,
Waco, Texas.*

6. The finish.

7. Lynching at Houston, Texas.

8. Florida lynching—1928.

9. A wholesale hanging. Four at a time.

10. Burned at the stake, Conroy, Texas.

11. *White mob with its Negro victim before the lynching.*

12. *Negro burned at the stake in Memphis, Tennessee.*

13. White mob exulting over its dead victim. Burned to death in Mississippi.

14. Negro stoned to death by whites in Chicago race riot.

15. Negro residence in North Side Chicago, after a crowd of whites had visited the section. Chicago race riot.

16. Ruins of colored school building, Red Bank, N. J., set fire by whites as a sequel to race war at Carteret, N. J.

LYNCH law is the method by which discrimination and segregation are enforced against recalcitrant members of the black race. Negroes who recognize their position of inferiority without question, who follow the white man's lead, who accept his judgments, and adhere to his decisions, take the wages which he offers and work the hours which he prescribes, have little trouble.

But woe to the Negro who transgresses the code that the white man proclaims! Usually there are no laws under which Negroes can be adequately punished for being "fresh" Negroes. The color line is more often drawn by vigilantes and local "law and order" men than by state statutes and constitutions. In fact, law and constitution accord the Negro equal rights as an American citizen. Lynching bees keep him in his place as a member of a subjugated, exploited race.

Mob law plays a role on every frontier. It is the agency by means of which the dominant group in a new community protects its interests and enforces its will.

White mob law in its dealings with Negroes has continued past the political and economic frontier to the frontier of race relations. It is the means by which the dominant white population of the United States, and particularly of the South, forces its will upon those members of the inferior black population who dare to question or to threaten white supremacy.

Mob rule in the case of Negroes ordinarily takes the form of lynching.

An American lynching is in many cases a public spectacle, which in its dramatic effects ranks with bull fights and Roman gladiatorial contests. Lynchings are frequently advertised in advance and staged in public places. Among the thousands who witness them are men, women and children.

Henry Lowry, a Negro about forty years of age, was lynched in Arkansas under conditions which typify the lynching practice as it has developed in the United States.

Lowry, with his wife and a six-year-old daughter were living on the farm of O. T. Craig, a large planter in Mississippi County, Arkansas. Lowry was rated an honest, hard-working and inoffensive Negro.

Craig, the planter, was an extensive land owner. He and his sons controlled the political as well as the economic life of the neighborhood.

As Christmas approached, Lowry, the Negro, asked Craig for a "settlement." He had been working about two years for the white planter, and it was said that Lowry was intending to move and wanted to know where he stood financially. In the course of the discussion, Richard Craig, son of O. T. Craig, struck Lowry and told him that if he wanted a settlement he must come some other day.

On Christmas day Lowry went again to the Craig house. The Craigs were at dinner and as Lowry walked up to the house, Bessie, the cook, entered the dining room reporting that Lowry had come back. When Lowry reached the porch he stated that he had come again to ask for a settlement. O. T. Craig ordered him off the place and threw a billet of wood, which struck Lowry. At the same time, Dick Craig, one of the sons, who had the reputation, among the Negroes, of being a "bad man," came out on the porch and as Lowry was backing off, shot him. It was then that Lowry pulled his gun and shot, killing O. T. Craig and his married daughter, and wounding both sons.

Lowry escaped from Arkansas and was arrested in El Paso, Texas, where he was held by the police until two deputy sheriffs arrived to take him to Arkansas.

An hour before the train bearing Lowry and the two deputy sheriffs reached Sardis, Mississippi, half a dozen travel-stained automobiles entered the little town. The *Memphis Press* of Wednesday, January 26, 1921, described their doings as follows:

> "Several men alighted from each auto, and went to the Illinois Central depot.
>
> " 'We are here to take that Negro off the train and carry him back to Wilson, Ark.,' the leader of the mob said as he approached Night Marshal W. E. Johnson, 'and we hope we won't have to cause any trouble here.'
>
> "The moment the train stopped each man drew a revolver and the leader boarded the Negro coach, followed closely by the others. Not a word was spoken.
>
> "Lowry was handcuffed to Deputy Greer, who was asleep, while Deputy Dixon stood guard.
>
> "Approaching them from behind, the mob members seized the deputies and disarmed them. One of them took the handcuff keys from Deputy Dixon's pocket and released Deputy Greer's wrist.
>
> "With the Negro between them, they filed out of the coach, leaving the officers behind."

The *Memphis News Scimitar* in its Final City Edition on Wednesday afternoon carried the following headlines: "Lowry Lynchers Announce Program; Negro to Pay Mob's Penalty for Crime."

The *Memphis Press* on the same evening in its Home Edition carried a heading extending across the entire front page: "May Lynch Three to Six Negroes This Evening." The leading story which occupied the center of the front page of the paper was: "Lowry Nears Tree

on Which It Is Planned to Hang Him; Taken Thru
Memphis Today." The story began:

> "While five of their number detoured around
> Memphis in a closed automobile with Henry Lowry,
> negro murderer, who is to be lynched at Nodena,
> Ark., tonight, other alleged members of the mob
> which took him from officers at Sardis, Miss., early
> this morning, came to Memphis and dined at Hotel
> Peabody today."

The Home Edition of the *Memphis Press* on Thursday
(the following day) carried a heading across the front
page: "Kill Negro By Inches." The story written from
the scene of the lynching by a *Memphis Press* reporter
described the incident as follows:

> "More than 500 persons stood by and looked on
> while the Negro was slowly burned to a crisp. A
> few women were scattered among the crowd of Ar-
> kansas planters, who directed the gruesome work
> of avenging the death of O. T. Craig and his
> daughter, Mrs. C. O. Williamson.
>
> "Not once did the slayer beg for mercy despite
> the fact that he suffered one of the most horrible
> deaths imaginable. With the Negro chained to a
> log, members of the mob placed a small pile of
> leaves around his feet. Gasoline was then poured
> on the leaves, and the carrying out of the death
> sentence was under way.
>
> "Inch by inch the Negro was fairly cooked to
> death. Every few minutes fresh leaves were tossed
> on the funeral pyre until the blaze had passed the
> Negro's waist. As the flames were eating away his
> abdomen, a member of the mob stepped forward

and saturated the body with gasoline. It was then only a few minutes until the Negro had been reduced to ashes.

"Even after the flesh had dropped away from his legs and the flames were leaping toward his face, Lowry retained consciousness. Not once did he whimper or beg for mercy. Once or twice he attempted to pick up the hot ashes in his hands and thrust them in his mouth in order to hasten death. . . ."

Evidently, from the reports, the bad state of the roads alone prevented the lynchers from reaching Marion and Blytheville in order to lay their hands on Morris Jenkins and J. T. Williams, both of whom were accused of assisting Lowry in making his escape immediately after he shot Craig and his daughter.

The lynching of Lowry is one of the many instances in which widespread newspaper publicity was given to the event more than twenty-four hours before it actually occurred. Although the leading newspapers of Memphis were carrying scare headlines, no effective measures were taken to prevent the lynching.

All of the evidence indicates that the plans for the lynching were very carefully laid and that hundreds of persons participated, directly or indirectly, in carrying the plans into effect.

The *Crisis*, for December, 1926 (pp. 72 ff.) gives the complete story of a South Carolina lynching. Sam Lowman and his family moved from Saluda County to a farm near Aiken, South Carolina, in 1924. A few months later a mob of robed and hooded Klansmen went to the Lowman house, called Demon, a twenty-two-year-old son, to the door, and gave him a severe whipping. Two weeks later Sheriff Howard of Aiken was advised in an anonymous letter that Sam Lowman was selling whiskey.

The Sheriff, accompanied by three deputies, all in civilian clothes, started in the direction of the Lowman home.

As the sheriff and his deputies approached the house, Annie Lowman, the fifty-five-year-old mother and her daughter Bertha were working in the yard. The daughter called her mother's attention to the approach of the four white men. Both women then started for the house. The white men saw them, drew their revolvers and began running toward the house in order to surround it. The Sheriff caught up with Bertha Lowman at the back steps, struck her in the mouth and ordered her to stand back. Mrs. Lowman, seeing her daughter was being attacked, picked up an axe and started to her assistance. She was shot dead by one of the deputy sheriffs.

The son Demon, and Clarence, a fifteen-year-old cousin, heard the shooting and ran toward the house. Demon got a revolver and Clarence a shot gun. Both sides then opened fire. In the course of the struggle, the Sheriff was killed. Bertha was shot three times and both boys were wounded.

There were rumors of lynching and the five Lowmans who had been arrested were taken to the penitentiary at Columbia.

The shooting occurred on April 25, 1925. On May 4, the Lowmans were indicted and tried on May 12. The two boys were sentenced to death and Bertha to life imprisonment. The case was appealed and the conviction set aside by a higher court.

In October, 1926, the local Judge, after hearing an argument by the attorneys for the Lowmans, directed a verdict of "Not Guilty" for Demon and ordered new trials for Clarence and Bertha.

"An hour after Judge Lanham delivered his decision a white man in Columbia was talking with his lawyer.

" 'I am sorry,' the client said, rising, 'but I will have to finish talking this over with you some other time.'

" 'What's your hurry?' the lawyer asked.

" 'Got to go over to Aiken right away.'

" 'What's going to happen there, and why are you in such a hurry?'

" 'They are going to lynch three niggers .over there to-night. Don't you want to come along?' " (Walter White, "Shambles of South Carolina," *Crisis*, December, 1926, p. 74.)

That night members of an organized mob secured access to the Aiken jail, opened the cells in which the three Lowmans were confined and took them in automobiles toward the spot which had been determined upon for the lynching. Clarence Lowman, fifteen, jumped from the car in which he was riding. He was shot down, a rope was taken from under the rear seat, one end of it was attached to Clarence's body and the other fastened to the rear axle. The journey was then resumed with the boy's body dragging along behind the car.

A thousand people had gathered at a tourist camp about a mile and a half from the town. The three Negroes were lined up and told to run. They started and as they did so they were shot in the back. "The two boys were dead; the woman was not. She thrashed about on the ground, begging piteously for life. 'She's bleating like a goat,' one of the mob members laughed derisively as he said it. The sight was too much for some of the mob and they turned their heads away. Others less tender-hearted fired shot after shot at the squirming figure. At last one bullet found a vital spot, a spasmodic quiver and the body was still."

Another form of torture was reported when Jim McIlherron, a Negro who shot and killed two white men, was tortured with a red hot crow bar and then burned to death before a crowd of approximately 2,000 persons among whom were men, women and children.

"McIlherron, who was badly wounded and unable to walk, was carried to the scene of the murder, where preparation for a funeral pyre was begun.

"The captors proceeded to a spot about a quarter of a mile from the railroad station and prepared the death fire. The crowd followed and remained throughout the horrible proceedings. The Negro was led to a hickory tree, to which they chained him. After securing him to the tree a fire was laid. A short distance away another fire was kindled, and into it was put an iron bar to heat.

"When the bar became red hot a member of the mob jabbed it toward the Negro's body. Crazed with fright, the black grabbed hold of it, and as it was pulled through his hands the atmosphere was filled with the odor of burning flesh. This was the first time the murderer gave evidence of his will being broken. Scream after scream rent the air. As the hot iron was applied to various parts of his body his yells and cries for mercy could be heard in the town.

"After torturing the Negro several minutes one of the masked men poured coal oil on his feet and trousers and applied a match to the pyre. As the flames rose, enveloping the black's body, he begged that he be shot. Yells of derision greeted his request. The angry flames consumed his clothing and little blue blazes shot upward from his burning hair before he lost consciousness. (*Chattanooga Daily Times. Crisis*, April, 1918, p. 270.)

A correspondent of the *Memphis News Scimitar* wrote the following description of a lynching which took place in the autumn of 1925:

"I watched an angry mob chain him to an iron stake. I watched them pile wood around his helpless body. I watched them pour gasoline on this wood. And I watched three men set this wood on fire. I stood in a crowd of 600 people as the flames gradually crept nearer and nearer to the helpless Negro. I watched the blaze climb higher and higher, encircling him without mercy. I heard his cry of agony as the flames reached him and set his clothing on fire.

"'Oh, God! Oh, God!' he shouted. 'I didn't do it. Have Mercy!' The blaze leaped higher. The Negro struggled. He kicked the chain loose from his ankles but it held his waist and neck against the iron post that was becoming red with the intense heat.

"'Have mercy, I didn't do it. I didn't do it!' He shouted again and again. . . .

"Soon he became quiet. There was no doubt that he was dead. The flames jumped and leaped above his head. An odor of burning flesh reached my nostrils. I felt suddenly sickened. Through the leaping blaze I could see the Negro sagging and supported by the chains.

"When the first odor of the baking flesh reached the mob there was a slight stir. Several men moved nervously.

"'Let's finish it up,' someone said.

"Instantly about 12 men stepped from the crowd.

They piled wood on the fire that was already blazing high. The Negro was dead, but more wood was piled on the flames. They jumped higher and higher. Nothing could be seen now for the blaze encircled everything.

"Then the crowd walked away. In the vanguard of the mob I noticed a woman. She seemed to be rather young, yet it is hard to tell about women of her type, strong and healthy, apparently a woman of the country. She walked with a firm, even stride. She was beautiful in a way.

"The crowd walked slowly away.

" 'I'm hungry,' someone complained.   'Let's get something to eat.' "   (*Crisis*, November, 1925, pp. 41-2.)

From 1885 to 1927, according to figures published in the *World Almanac*, 3,226 Negroes were lynched in the United States. During the same period 1,047 white persons were lynched in the United States. From 1885 to 1889 Negro lynchings ranged from 71 to 95 per year. In 1891, 121 Negroes were lynched. From 1891 until 1895 Negro lynchings ranged from 112 to 155 (1892). Since 1901 there has been no single year in which as many as 100 Negroes were lynched. The lowest numbers on record were 16 lynchings in 1924 and 17 in 1925.

Thirty Years of Lynching in the United States—1889 to 1918 is the title of a pamphlet published by the National Association for the Advancement of Colored People, in April, 1919. During these 30 years the total number of white and colored persons lynched in the United States was 3,224. Of this number 702 were white and 2,522 were Negroes. Among the 2,522 Negroes lynched, 2,472 were males and 50 were females.

The National Association for the Advancement of Colored People has published a record of lynching for each year since 1918. During 1927, 21 men were lynched—7 in Mississippi, 3 in Tennessee, 3 in Arkansas, 2 in Florida, 1 in California, 1 in Kentucky, 1 in Louisiana, 1 in Missouri, 1 in North Carolina and 1 in Texas. Three of those lynched, all of them Negroes, were burned to death.

Most of the Negro lynchings have taken place in the South. During the 30 years between 1889 and 1918 the North reported 219 lynchings, the South, 2,834 and the West, 156. Georgia leads the list of states with 386 lynchings; followed by Mississippi with 373; Texas with 335; Louisiana with 313; Alabama with 276; Arkansas with 214; Tennessee with 296; Florida with 178 and Kentucky with 169.

There is a general belief that most lynchings occur because of attacks on women. The figures show that this is not the case. Among the 2,522 Negroes lynched between 1889 and 1918, 900 were charged with murder; 477 with rape, 237 with attacks upon women; 253 with other crimes against the person; 210 with crimes against property and 303 with miscellaneous crimes. One hundred and forty-two cases of lynching are classified as "absence of crime" with this explanation, "Under this head are listed such causes as 'testifying against whites'; 'suing whites'; 'wrong man lynched'; etc."

Not the least remarkable of the various aspects of American lynching is the number of women lynched. Between 1889 and 1925 there are 90 instances of lynching of women. Nine took place in Alabama; 9 in Arkansas; 8 in Georgia; 16 in Mississippi; 6 in South Carolina; 7 in Tennessee; 11 in Texas. The charges against these women were murder, implication in murder, resisting arrest, relationship to criminals, disorderly conduct, etc.

The National Association for the Advancement of Colored People has recently led a movement, which has had widespread support, to secure Federal legislation against lynching. While a number of states have passed anti-lynching laws, local sentiment generally protects the lynchers. The *Daily News* of Jackson, Mississippi, is quoted by the *Crisis* of November, 1925, page 42, as follows:

> "For the first time in the history of this state, so far as is known, a mob member has publicly admitted his guilt, and issued a statement concerning the affair.
>
> "William N. Bradshaw, of Union county, admits he was a member of the mob that searched for the guilty Negro, and declares that 'Gov. Whitfield won't have a lick of luck with any investigation of the burning of Jim Ivy.'
>
> " 'And furthermore,' he continued, 'not an officer in Union county or any of the neighboring counties will point out any members of the crowd. Why, if he did, the best thing for him to do would be to jump into an airplane headed for Germany—quick.
>
> " 'Sure, the officers know who were there. Everybody down there knows everybody else. . . .
>
> "Even one of the judges down there said he 'didn't believe in mob law except in a few cases and this was one of them' and that 'he'd have gone to the burning if it hadn't been bad policy.' . . .
>
> "A coroner's jury which investigated the lynching returned a verdict that Ivy came to his death 'at the hands of a mob, the members of which are unknown.' "

Indictments have been returned in some recent cases of lynching. Generally, however, no attempt is made to punish the lynchers, even in states which have laws specifically prohibiting lynching. There is no question of identification. Pictures of the lynchings and of the mob are sold on the streets. Local sentiment is behind the practice and the local judicial machinery is paralyzed.

A student of American lynchings sums the matter up in these words: "There is usually more or less public approval, or supposed favorable public sentiment, behind a lynching. . . . A lynching may be defined as an illegal and summary execution at the hands of a mob, or a number of persons, who have in some degree the public opinion of the community behind them." (Cutler, *Lynch Law*, p. 276.)

Friction between whites and Negroes in the United States occasionally leads to race riots or race wars. While such outbreaks have occurred at intervals for many years, a number of them were concentrated in the period from 1917 to 1920, and in those parts of the country to which there had been extensive and recent Negro migrations. One of the most disastrous of these race wars took place in Chicago during the summer of 1919. It was described in a very extensive report, *The Negro in Chicago*. (The Chicago Commission on Race Relations, Chicago, University of Chicago Press, 1922.) In the course of this race war 38 persons, including 15 whites, were killed; 537 persons, including 178 whites were injured, and about 1,000 individuals were rendered homeless through the depredations of the mobs.

The Chicago race riot started casually enough. Whites and Negroes were bathing in Lake Michigan on two beaches in the neighborhood of Twenty-ninth Street, South Side. The races kept apart, the whites using the northern beach and the Negroes the southern. There was no official segregation, but the separation took place by common consent.

Sunday afternoon, July 27, four Negroes walked through the white section of the bathing beach and started into the water. White men ordered them to leave. There was a discussion and some stones were thrown. The Negroes went back to their own beach, returned with reinforcements and the conflict continued.

A seventeen year old Negro boy had left the Negro bathing beach and was swimming opposite the beach on which the whites were bathing. During the stone throwing he apparently became frightened and instead of swimming back to the Negro beach, got hold of a piece of wood and stayed out of stone range in deep water. A white man started to swim toward the Negro boy. The latter let go his hold of the piece of wood, took a few strokes and went down. There was no evidence that the Negro boy was hit by a stone. Several Negroes, however, charged that he had been struck by a stone and pointed out a white man who had been throwing at him. The white policeman refused to arrest the white man charged with stoning the Negro boy.

Whites and Negroes joined in diving for the boy's body. There was excited talk and a crowd of Negroes gathered as news spread that a Negro boy had been stoned to death. A group of police appeared and in the course of a conflict with the crowd of Negroes a Negro policeman was shot by a member of the crowd. The Negro policeman drew his own revolver and killed his assailant.

That Sunday afternoon the Negro crowd at Twenty-ninth Street beat 4 white men, stabbed 5 others and shot 1. Further west during the evening white crowds beat 27 Negroes, stabbed 7 and shot 4.

Monday morning Chicago went to work as usual, but during the afternoon Negroes on their way home from work were dragged from the cars and mobbed by whites. During these attacks 4 Negroes and 1 white were killed and 30 Negro men were severely beaten.

Negro mobs were also active. In the course of the

evening they stabbed 6 white men, shot 5 others, severely beat 9 and killed 4. On the same evening there was a clash with the police who fired into the mob. Four Negroes were killed and many injured. "At this point Monday night, both whites and Negroes showed signs of panic. Each race grouped by itself. Small mobs began systematically, in various neighborhoods, to terrorize and kill." (*Negro in Chicago*, p. 6.)

White gangs raided Negro territory. Automobiles were used for the purpose. They were driven through the Negro quarters at high speed, the occupants firing indiscriminately as they passed. As the auto raids grew more frequent, Negroes replied by firing on all cars passing through their territory. Riot conditions continued on Tuesday, and on Wednesday the Mayor of Chicago reluctantly called the State Militia to his aid. Troops remained on duty until August 8.

Chicago is the second most populous city in the United States. The Negro section of the south side with its population of approximately 125,000 is one of the most highly concentrated Negro quarters in any city of the United States. Negroes had been migrating into Chicago during the early period of the war. Toward the end of the war, however, with high wages and labor demand, the number of Negroes greatly increased. Negroes were pressing into white men's jobs and into white neighborhoods. The friction was intensified by the use of Negroes as strikebreakers. Thus the general dislodgement provided the stimulus out of which race conflict arose.

Recent race conflicts in the United States are thus analyzed by Reuter: "The war, in a number of places, brought the inter-racial situation to a premature climax. The increased mobility, the improved economic position, and the army experience of the Negroes stimulated the development of a race conscious solidarity. On the part of the whites an increased hatred of race was an integral part of the war-time intolerance. There were a number of armed conflicts resulting in bloodshed and the destruction of property. Even more frequent were the occasions where riots were narrowly averted or were suppressed before they assumed the proportion or duration of racial war. In the year 1919 serious riots occurred in seven cities: Chicago, Illinois; Elaine, Arkansas; Charleston, South Carolina; Knoxville, Tennessee; Longview, Texas; Omaha, Nebraska; and Washington, D. C. In the following year similar riots took place at Duluth, Minnesota; Independence, Kansas; and Ococe, Florida. In 1921 there were riots of serious proportions at Springfield, Ohio, and Tulsa, Oklahoma. Other serious race conflicts occurred at Coatesville, Pennsylvania; Springfield, Illinois; Chester, Pennsylvania; Rosewood, Florida; Johnstown, Pennsylvania, and East St. Louis, Illinois." (Reuter, *The American Race Problem*, p. 418.)

Relations between American Negroes and American whites occupy a frontier of conflict which is beyond the pale of organized society. Some of these relations are regulated by law, but for the most part the subject Negro race is held in its subject position by the dominant white race through organized violence. In the case of individuals, lynchings are conducted by organized mobs. Larger social issues lead to race wars in which white mobs indiscriminately wreck and burn Negro dwellings and beat and kill Negroes.

These organized lawless mob attacks by whites on Negroes usually go unpunished. Law enforcement in the United States is an exclusive function of the dominant white race, and thus far the dominant race has not hesitated to break the law when any need arose for keeping Negroes in their place.

20: A SUBJECT RACE

NEGROES in the important centers of American economic life are a subject race. They are racially segregated and treated as racial inferiors.

Economic power lies in the hands of the whites. They are the job owners. When it comes to a choice between various jobs the Negroes are discriminated against; the whites are favored. The whites through their domination of business machinery control the economic surplus. Thus the whole economic field from job ownership to the control of surplus rests with the whites.

From this field, and particularly from the higher positions in it, Negroes are rigidly, almost automatically excluded—they remain the underdogs. Millions of Negro men and women continue through their whole lives to do the humblest and lowest paid work without any hope or possibility of advancement, or even of wages or salaries commensurate with those paid to whites in similar circumstances. "The Negro of our times carries even more heavily the burden of his racial descent than did the Jew of an earlier period; and the intellectual and moral qualities required to insure success to the Negro are infinitely greater than those demanded of the white, and will be greater, the stricter the segregation of the Negro community." (Ovington, *Half a Man*, p. viii.) Duncan writes that the Negro masses are being held to "the lowest, most menial occupations. The Negro has room at the bottom but no fixed industrial status." (*Changing Race Relationships*, p. 82.)

Some effort has been made to prove that Negroes are mentally, physically and racially inferior to whites: therefore less efficient: therefore less entitled to income or to occupational promotion. This propaganda has been vigorously promulgated through the North during the period of active Negro migration. Much of it has its origin in college classrooms and laboratories.

Such arguments avoid the main issue.

Negroes are not exploited and discriminated against economically because of their inferior capacity. If inferior capacity were the test, the whites would distinguish between Negroes in proportion to their capacity to perform the particular task in hand. Those Negroes who were competent to perform the task would be selected for it; those Negroes who were unable to perform the task would be rejected because of their lack of competence.

Economic discrimination against the Negro rests on no such basis.

From slave days certain Negroes have displayed unusual capacities in all of the important lines of human endeavor. There have been highly gifted Negro singers, poets, actors, logicians, scientists, organizers; but these outstanding leaders of the Negro race have been treated by the whites not as poets, scientists and organizers, but as Negroes—that is, as members of an inferior race.

Negroes in the United States are discriminated against economically because they are Negroes, irrespective of their personal capacities. This is so universally true both North and South that it is virtually axiomatic.

While the whites continue, as a race, to own the sources of economic power with which the blacks must work in order to live, a definite consciousness of whiteness will remain among members of the exploiting race and an equally definite consciousness of blackness will be forced upon members of the exploited race. The present strained race relations must continue no matter what the qualities or the fate of individual Negroes may be.

Negroes make up the largest single segregated group of American mass labor. While they remain segregated and while the ownership and control of economic opportunity remains in the hands of the whites, the Negroes must inevitably continue to be the object of white exploitation.

American Negroes are a subject race economically. Economic subjection and exploitation are reflected in political subordination.

Politically, American Negroes hold no position of importance anywhere in the United States. Negroes are not elected to important public offices even where Negroes are in the overwhelming majority. Nowhere do strategic public appointments go to Negroes. "Everywhere in the South the whites are in political control. Even in the Black Belt where the Negro population outnumbers many times that of the white race, all the offices, with a few unimportant exceptions, are filled by white men. With all the millions of Negroes in the South there is not one who holds state or county office or occupies a seat in the legislature and, except in a few small towns and villages inhabited almost wholly by Negroes, there is not to be found a colored mayor, member of the municipal council, justice of the peace or even a policemen. Negroes rarely sit on juries, they are not allowed to serve in the militia and of course they are never found on registration or election boards." (Garner, *Southern Politics since the Civil War*, p. 377.)

Despite legal and constitutional guarantees the Negro masses do not vote. Even where the Negroes are able to establish a complete racial solidarity and seek to formulate demands at the polls, they have no means of enforcing their decisions upon the members of the white exploiting class.

White men in the United States own economically and dominate politically. The Negro voter is perhaps more of an inferior than the Negro worker. At least large numbers of Negroes are able to earn their living, even if it be a meager one, by their labor. With a few minor exceptions in the great centers of American Negro population, the Negro masses do not and cannot vote.

Economic and political subjugation are reflected in the Negro's position of social inferiority. No matter what his personal attainments may be, the Negro cannot make a place for himself socially in any part of the United States. He cannot mingle with whites on a basis of equality in private homes. He is discriminated against and segregated in public institutions. He is a social outcast against whom the white ruling class directs an incessant vigorous propaganda, the object of which is to establish and maintain a sense of racial inferiority.

South of the Mason and Dixon line where the great masses of American Negroes live, they have been treated as a subject race from the early days of slavery. During recent years with the migration of Negro labor into industrial centers of both North and South, the same racial discrimination and segregation are appearing in the North.

Racial pressure on the Negro has risen as he has become more articulate and active. This was particularly noticeable during and immediately after the world war in which millions of Negroes participated with the firm belief that the winning of the war would mean greater racial opportunities.

Negro-white relations in the United States were recently summarized for the *World Tomorrow* by Charles S. Johnson under the rather questionable general title: "Recent Gains in American Civilization." Mr. Johnson's article shows very clearly that the pressure on the Negroes is increasing.

He begins by calling attention to the absence of strict segregation in slave days, when Negroes habitually lived with and worked with and for their white masters!

◆ 216 ◆

Then, with the Reconstruction Period passed, the whites put the screws on the Negroes:

1. "Between 1881 and 1907 all the Southern States enacted laws separating the races on railroad cars, street cars and schools, and excluding Negroes from jury service and the primaries." (p. 14.)

2. "The practice of lynching took on a new impetus; it became a hybrid sport-vengeance." (p. 14.)

3. "More than a million Negroes moved from the South, from agriculture to industry. The increased proportions of Negroes brought limitations of their privileges in the North." There were race riots. "Economic rivalry was fiercest at precisely the moment Negroes were moving deepest into the web of industrialism." (p. 14.)

4. "Seventeen cities in the North within the past four years have been conspicuous for clashes in housing, resistance to the 'invasion of white neighborhoods,' and vehement charges of 'property depreciation' have grown as the Negro population spread. Segregation instead of lessening, has tended to increase." (p. 15.)

5. "Atlanta, Georgia, and Charleston, South Carolina, have put forth bills to prevent Negro barbers from handling white trade. The growing labor consciousness of the South is barring Negroes from trades. Northern Universities have introduced limitations on Negro students and some have quietly barred them entirely. Agitation for separate Negro schools in the North has met with some success."

6. "Personal privileges have been limited for Negroes in every city where the population has become large, making it appear to many, that no measurable gains have been made at all in race relations:

rather that these relations merely have been levelled over a wider area." (P. 15.) (*World Tomorrow*, January, 1928.)

Black America is the source from which the white ruling class of the United States proposes to draw an important part of its mass labor power. Upon this mass labor the white rulers make two demands: (1) it must work cheap; (2) it must do what it is told. These demands mean low standards of living and the acceptance, by the blacks, of the social code prescribed by the whites.

The white ruling class is in a position to enforce these demands. They hold the economic power. They have a monopoly of politics. They dominate the educational and propaganda machinery. They are favored by a tradition of inferiority inherited from slave days. With comparative ease, therefore, twelve million American Negroes are being held in a position of racial subjugation where their mass labor power can be secured at the lowest wages and with the greatest net profit to the whites.

III: THE NEGRO STRUGGLE FOR FREEDOM

21: THE BLACK MAN'S BURDEN

LIKE every other oppressed race, American Negroes have struggled for freedom and self-expression. This struggle has continued since earliest slave days. Individual Negroes have tried to escape the implications of race subjugation. Negroes in the mass have sought to free themselves from exploitation and to win for their race the opportunities enjoyed by the whites.

Slave revolts occurred frequently. Only in the West Indies were they successful. Throughout the slave territory of the United States they were suppressed, and fearful punishments were meted out to the ringleaders in these mass efforts toward Negro emancipation.

During the early days of slavery, before the white slave-owning class had thoroughly organized itself, slave revolts actually menaced white domination. With the more complete organization of the white slave owners, however, the later slave revolts were never more than sporadic local efforts, directed against particular slave owners rather than against the whole system of slavery.

The *Negro Year Book* for 1925-1926 (pp. 213-215) briefly describes the more important slave insurrections. The editor notes that "some 25 insurrections of slaves took place in the United States prior to the American Revolution." (p. 213.) After the revolution, and with the growing wealth and importance of the Southern planters, slave revolts became less and less vital as a factor in Southern public life.

At the outbreak of the Civil War, with the greatly increased wealth and organization of the Southern slave-holding class, the American Negroes seemed further than ever from emancipation through their own efforts. Four million of them were slaves—the physical property of white men. The half million free Negroes owned little property, had virtually no political rights, and were treated as a subject race socially.

The Civil War of 1861-1865 did for the Negroes what the Negroes could not at that period have done for themselves. In 1863, as a war measure, President Lincoln by a stroke of the pen declared all of the slaves free.

Although the Civil War was not fought primarily to liberate Negro slaves, the Proclamation of Emancipation and the Thirteenth Amendment of the United States Constitution prohibiting slavery were two of its most important results. Both of these measures were enforced, by an industrial "free-labor" North upon an agricultural "slave-labor" South. Emancipation, the amended constitution and the Reconstruction Era, during which the Southern States remained under a Northern military dictatorship, were all a part of the social process by which the business-controlled North forced industrialization upon the planter-controlled South. In the course of this social transformation the Negro slaves were liberated and granted full citizenship rights.

Having won the war, the business class of the North took up the task of reconstruction. Economically, reconstruction meant the industrialization of the South. Politically it meant the readmission of the Southern States into the Union on conditions acceptable to the victorious North. Two of these conditions were the Fourteenth and Fifteenth Amendments to the United States Constitution.

The Fourteenth and Fifteenth Amendments were ostensibly designed to guarantee civil rights, including the right to vote, to Negroes. Practically, they have been utilized to protect corporate interests and to solidify and advance the economic position of the white ruling class of the United States. During reconstruction days, however, the fight which centered around these amendments was based on the assumption that their enforcement would not only give Negroes the right to vote, but would likewise guarantee them the other civil rights enumerated in the first ten amendments to the United States Constitution and in the bills of rights incorporated in the constitutions of the individual states.

This was paper liberation. At the end of the Civil War there were about five million Negroes in the United States. Most of them were illiterate. Few of them had property. Only here and there was there a Negro business or professional man. The great mass of emancipated Negroes were field hands and servants who had had no training or experience aside from that which slavery on Southern plantations had offered.

Since the Negroes were propertyless and jobless a Freedmen's Bureau was organized to assist them in securing land and in establishing an economic basis for their newly gained freedom. The Freedmen's Bureau also did some pioneer work in the direction of Negro education. At best, however, it was a tool of Northern economic and political interests that was employed against the wishes of the white South. In the Black Belt its work was never effective.

The Northern whites, in their effort to establish a free labor system, abolished slavery, gave the Negroes constitutional and legal guarantees of civil rights, and provided a federal government department, the ostensible purpose of which was the advancement of Negro interests.

The Negroes, on their side, migrated from the more densely populated and older portions of the South into the newly developing cotton territory of the Southwest. There was also an inconsiderable migration from the plantations to the industrial cities both South and North.

The Negro masses twenty years after the end of the Civil War were still working the land; for the most part they were still bound to the land through some form of peonage or debt control; most of them were property-less; they were illiterate. Legally, they had ceased to be slaves. Practically, they still made up a working class bound to the soil and exploited by white land owners.

The victory of the North, in 1865, resulted, according to the history books, in "the freeing of the Slaves." Freeing from what? For what?

Theoretically, and legally, the Negroes were freed from slavery.

Practically, and economically, the Negroes were still under the necessity of making a living on land owned by Southern white men.

Negroes obtained no new economic status as a result of the Emancipation Proclamation. Fifty years passed before they made any effective gesture in the direction of industry. Reconstruction left them land workers and house servants; serfs in fact, if not in law.

Economically, politically, socially, Black America still carried the burdens of subjugation and exploitation after the Proclamation of Emancipation and the defeat of the South in the Civil War. Theoretically the slaves became freemen. Actually they continued to work on the same land, often for the same master, and under conditions rendered doubly onerous through war losses and war chaos.

22: THE FARCE OF POLITICAL DEMOCRACY

NORTHERN industrialists, as part of their program for converting the slave Negro into a free Negro, amended the Constitution of the United States in such a way that the Negro was enfranchised. Advocates of democracy hailed this achievement as a measure of Negro emancipation. Many of the Negro leaders themselves regarded politics as the avenue along which freedom must be won.

Believers in the possibility of Negro emancipation through political action were soon disillusioned, particularly in State and local elections. In all of the Southern State legislatures there were Negro representatives and senators. In South Carolina, the legislature in 1868-1869 contained 24 white and 9 Negro senators and 48 white and 76 Negro representatives. In the lower house of the legislature the Negroes were therefore in a large majority.

Tables were rapidly turned, however. In 1873-4 the South Carolina lower house contained 63 whites and 61 Negroes. In 1876, 70 whites and 54 Negroes. In other Southern states, similar reductions were made in Negro representation.

The first Negro Congressman was elected in 1869; the last in 1899. In 1873, five were elected; in 1875, six. This was the peak of Negro representation. After 1879 there was never more than one Negro representative in Congress.

As Northern military control was withdrawn from the South the process of disfranchising the Negro was begun. For a time Southern whites contented themselves with terrorism as a means of disfranchising

Negroes. In 1890, Mississippi began a movement to legally exclude Negroes from the franchise.

Other Southern States immediately followed the lead of Mississippi. South Carolina in 1895, Louisiana in 1898, North Carolina in 1900, Alabama and Virginia in 1901 and Georgia in 1908, laid down legal restrictions under which the mass of Negroes were no longer eligible to vote. Laws or constitutional provisions which restrict Negro voting are now in force in Mississippi, South Carolina, Louisiana, North Carolina, Alabama, Virginia, Georgia and Oklahoma.

How do these laws operate? "The process is so complicated few Negroes themselves know definitely." (*Crisis*, June, 1925, p. 62.)

"Beginning with 1890, laws have been passed in various Southern States which today disfranchise approximately four million Negroes twenty-one years of age and over, over half of whom can read and write, and who own property which runs into the hundreds of millions." (*Crisis*, June, 1925, p. 62.) The editor of *The Crisis* then lists eight methods by which Negro disfranchisement is accomplished:

1. *Literacy*. Voters must be able to read and write.
2. *Property*. Voters must own a certain amount of property.
3. *Poll Tax*. The voter must have paid his poll tax within the year or for a number of years.
4. *Employment*. The voter must have regular employment.
5. *Army service*. Soldiers who fought in the Civil War or in certain other wars, or the descendants of such soldiers may vote.
6. *Reputation*. Persons of good reputation, who understand the duties of a citizen may vote.

7. *Grandfather clauses*. Persons who could vote before the Negroes were enfranchised or descendants of such persons may vote.

8. *Understanding clause*. Persons may vote who understand some selected clauses of the constitution and who can explain these clauses to the satisfaction of the registration officials.

Under these provisions any Negro voter who is objectionable to the white election officials may be disfranchised.

These eight methods of Negro disfranchisement are, however, relatively unimportant when compared with the "white primary." The white primary is legally the primary election of the Democratic Party. Any white elector who agrees to stand by the decisions of the primary is eligible to vote in the primary. Negroes, on the other hand, are seldom allowed to vote. Since the decisions of the primary are in effect the legal election, the exclusion of Negroes from the primary is really an exclusion from the election. The real political struggles in the South are the political struggles leading to the primary election. The election itself is usually a formality.

Where Southern Negroes, despite the obvious will of the ruling white class, persist in their efforts to vote, they are met with violence. The *Crisis*, (May, 1925, p. 41) reproduced a Florida election poster:

"BEWARE!

"Negro Citizens, as long as you keep your place, we will protect you,

BUT

BEWARE, the Klu-Klux-Klan is Again Alive! And Every NEGRO who approaches a polling place next Tuesday will be

A MARKED MAN.
This is a White man's country, boys, so save your
own life next Tuesday.
KLU KLUX KLAN
Miami Chapter
P. S. Don't think for a minute that we don't
know you. A white man will be at every polling
place with his book. Don't Get In That Book!"

A Southern white man from the Gulf Coast district
of Mississippi described the situation in his country by
saying, "We don't have Republican voters, and Negroes
don't vote the Democratic ticket." Asked what would
happen to Negroes who went to the polling place and
made an effort to vote on election day, he replied, "They
know better than to try."

Negroes in Northern industrial centers vote with
about the same freedom as other citizens. In the South,
however, where the great mass of Negroes live and work,
Negroes do not vote.

The year 1920 was both a census year and a presidential election year. W. E. B. DuBois, editor of the
Crisis, who took the occasion to compare the census
figures with the election figures, showed that:

1. The percentage of the total population who voted
   in the North and West ranged from 25.3 percent
   in the Middle Atlantic States to 34.5 percent in
   the Southwestern States. In the South, 9.7 percent
   of the population voted.

2. The percentage of voters who voted in the North
   and West ranged from 50.3 percent in New
   England to 70 percent in the Southwest. In the
   South 17.6 percent of the voters voted.

3. The percentage of population voting, by individual
   States was: South Carolina, 3.9 percent; Missis-

sippi, 4.6 percent; Georgia, 5.1 percent; Louisiana, 6.3 percent; Texas, 9.2 percent; Alabama, Arkansas, Virginia, 10 percent; New York, 27 percent; Illinois, 30 percent; Minnesota, 30 percent: California, 27 percent. (The *Crisis*, February, 1921, p. 158.)

The disfranchisement of Negroes is not new. South Carolina inserted the word "white" in the franchise law of 1716; Virginia disfranchised Negroes in 1762; Georgia, in 1761. Between the Revolution of 1776 and the Civil War of 1861, Southern Negroes generally did not vote. In Virginia, South Carolina, Florida and Alabama, the ballot was specifically limited to whites. Between 1835 and the Civil War Negroes were effectively disfranchised throughout the South. (Reuter, *The American Race Problem*, pp. 150-2.)

During Reconstruction Days the Negroes enjoyed a brief period of voting opportunity. "After 1876 the Negro vote ceased to be an item of importance to the state governments." (*Ibid.*, p. 152.)

Southern Negroes do not vote. Neither do they hold important political offices. A Negro lawyer from Virginia summed up the situation in his state by saying: "There is no Negro judge on the bench of Virginia. So far as I know there is not a single Negro police magistrate in Virginia. I do not believe that there is even a Negro attendant in any Virginia court." He added that this generalization was equally true for the entire South.

Participation in political activity is ordinarily a function of the ruling class. A temporary conflict within the ruling class, such as that which occurred at the time of the American Civil War, disrupts ruling class control. It was during this era of disruption or "Reconstruction" when a new economic system was being established in the South that the subject Negro race enjoyed a brief period of electoral opportunity. No sooner was the American white ruling class again substantially unified than it proceeded with the business of Negro disfranchisement.

Political power "spoils" an exploited class. Hence the white ruling class of the United States is excluding the Negroes from the enjoyment of "political democracy."

Intelligent American Negroes no longer expect emancipation through the franchise. The facts of history and contemporary American experience are alike against them. "It would be of no advantage to the Negro race today to send to Congress forty Negro Representatives on the pro rata basis of numbers, especially if they happened not to be especially well qualified. They would remain in Congress only so long as the American white people could devise some plan for eliminating them as they did during the Reconstruction period." (Woodson, *Century of Negro Migration*, pp. 181-2.)

The idea of Negro emancipation through the franchise and through political action has proved a delusion. Negro leadership which turned to politics has been lost to the Negro race and Negro mass energy which has supported Negro political action has wasted itself. The franchise and political action are not means of emancipation for an exploited class but are tools employed by ruling classes in the exercise of class power. Negroes who devote themselves to politics as a means of race emancipation are merely dissipating energy and helping to rivet the shackles more firmly.

2. *Negro school girl, Harlem, New York City.*

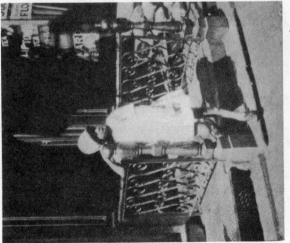

1. *With improved economic conditions, Negro children are better cared for. Negro girl, Harlem, New York City.*

3. A Negro family in Harlem, New York City, which has secured a higher standard of living.

4. A member of the Negro bourgeoisie of Harlem, New York City.

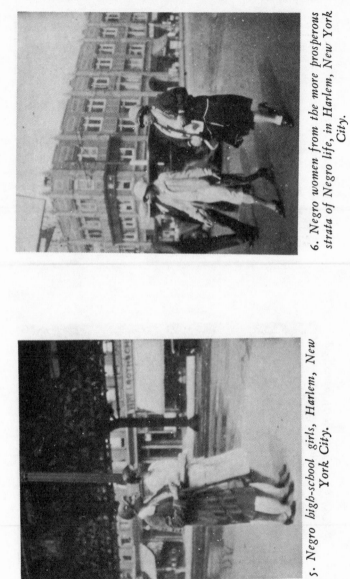

6. Negro women from the more prosperous strata of Negro life, in Harlem, New York City.

5. Negro high-school girls, Harlem, New York City.

7. *Negroes enter the professions. Two Negro preachers in Harlem, New York City.*

8. *Negroes share in law enforcement. Negro policemen, Harlem, New York City.*

9. Negroes engage in business. A garage owned and run by Negroes in Cleveland.

10. The president of a Negro finance corporation in his Chicago office.

11. Homes of prosperous Negroes in Chicago.

*12. The Stenographers Institute, a Negro business col-
lege in Philadelphia.*

14. The Dunbar apartments in Harlem, New York City, where 511 Negro families have escaped from the ugliness which ordinarily surrounds Negro life.

13. A Negro doll factory in Harlem which provides colored dolls for Negro children.

15. *Tuskegee University sends demonstration agents into the farming communities to teach modern agricultural methods. A lesson in culling poultry. Alabama.*

16. *Demonstration agent of Morgan County, Alavuma, teaching club boy how to select his seed corn.*

17. Founders Day at Spelman College, Atlanta, Ga.

18. A graduating class from Hampton University, June, 1928.

*19. Processional, Bennett College for Women, Greens-
boro, N. C.*

*20. A Negro inventor: Robert Blair, inventor of anti-
aircraft gun.*

22. *A Negro scientist, Dr. G. W. Carver.*

21. *A Negro woman chemist, Cleveland, Ohio.*

23. A Negro poet, Langston Hughes.

24. A Negro actor and singer, Paul Robeson.

26. Richard B. Moore, Secretary of the American Negro Labor Congress.

25. James Weldon Johnson, Secretary of the National Association for the Advancement of Colored People.

27. *American Negro Labor Congress.*

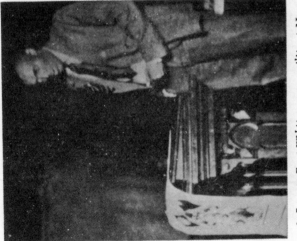

29. *Isaac Hawkins, organizer of District of the United Mine Workers' Union.*

28. *Lovett Fort Whiteman, a militant Negro labor leader, one of the organizers of the American Negro Labor Congress.*

30. Black and white miners striking together in the coal fields of Pennsylvania.

31. Black workers and white workers together for a free America!

23 : RUNAWAYS

WHILE some of the American Negro slaves were engaged in mass struggles, conspiracies and revolts aimed to liberate the Negro race, individual slaves ran away. They ran to the swamps of the South, where they were hunted like animals with bloodhounds and guns. They ran to the North along the "underground railway," escaped across the border into Canada, and were "free."

The runaway slaves in the swamps and everglades lived in constant terror of recapture and of the fearful punishments which were meted out to runaways. The Negroes who reached Canada were still Negroes. Legally they were free; racially their problem remained unsolved.

With the ending of slavery, the place of the runaway slave was taken by the individual Negro who sought through personal achievement to escape the implications of his membership in an exploited race. Gifted Negroes left behind the masses of their black fellows and became successful business men and women, successful professional men and women, successful creative artists.

Negro exploiters—land owners and business men—joined the ruling class of the United States economically. They placed themselves in a position where they could hire other human beings for profit; where they could live on the labor of their fellows. The Census of 1920 listed about 70,000 Negroes engaged in business enterprises. Some of the most important numerically were:

Restaurant and Lunch Room Keepers.. 7,511
Grocers 6,339
Truck Gardeners 6,242

Hucksters and Peddlers...................... 3,194

Butchers and Meat Dealers................. 3,009

Miscellaneous Retail Dealers................ 1,754

Pool Room Keepers 1,582

Undertakers 1,558

Contractors and Builders...................... 1,454

Real Estate Dealers 1,369

Junk Dealers 1,132

Hotel Keepers and Managers................. 1,020

American Negroes are operating 70,000 business enterprises. On its face this is a large number. Actually, however, the figure is far less impressive than it appears.

1. The total number of business concerns in the United States is given by Bradstreets as 2,258,423. Although Negroes make up one-tenth of the United States population, they control only 3 percent of its business concerns.

2. Most of these 70,000 Negro business concerns are engaged in retail trade and in personal service. Many of them serve Negroes largely or exclusively.

3. They do not include the basic industries or services —coal, iron and steel, chemicals, machinery, automobiles, food, packing, textiles, railroads.

4. Almost all Negro business in the United States is "small business." "Big business" remains a monopoly of the whites.

Negroes have also entered the professions. They have become lawyers, doctors, teachers, thus demonstrating their ability to match wits with members of the white ruling class of the United States.

The Occupational Census of 1920 reports 41,056 male Negroes and 39,127 female Negroes in professional groups, a total of 80,183 of the 2,143,889 listed occupationally by the Census as in the professional group. While the Negroes make up 10 percent of the United States population they supply only 3.6 percent of its professional people.

Among the male Negro professionals are 19,343 clergymen; 6,319 teachers; 3,752 musicians and teachers of music; 3,430 physicians and surgeons; 1,378 actors and showmen; 496 college presidents and professors. Both male and female Negro professional people are narrowly concentrated in a comparatively few occupations.

Negroes have entered the fields of creative art as writers, poets, singers, painters, sculptors. They have competed directly and in many cases successfully with white artists. Within the past twenty years American Negro poetry, music and literature have made a place for themselves not only in the United States but in various foreign countries. (Weatherford, *The Negro from Africa to America*, Chapter XV, "The Negro and Self Expression"; Reuter, *American Race Problem*, Chapter XII, "Negro in Literature, Art and Music.")

Individual Negro men and women have succeeded in business, in professions, in the arts. In these fields they have won positions of importance and distinction in competition with the whites and against comparatively great odds. They were handicapped in their efforts to gain an education; when they entered the world of competitive endeavor they found the hand of almost every man turned against them. As members of an "inferior" race they were reaching for rewards, ordinarily reserved for the successful members of the "superior" race. They were racial interlopers, and were treated accordingly.

Despite great obstacles, in the face of general opposition, after overcoming bitter prejudice, Negro business men, professionals and artists won distinction. Their talents and achievements cannot be successfully questioned.

But after these Negroes had struggled to positions of business, professional and artistic eminence, they were still black—excluded from social contact with the whites; barred from restaurants, theaters, hotels, sleeping cars; confronted on every side with reiterations of the inferiority implied in their blackness. Personal achievement does not relieve an American Negro of his chief handicap: his membership in an exploited race.

Even the "successful" Negroes have been unable to escape the racial disabilities which their Negro blood implies among the white ruling class of the United States. As for the Negro masses, despite the talent and achievement of a favored few, they remain the hewers of wood and drawers of water, doing the heavy, unskilled, dirty work of the United States.

One of the requisite means to the continuance of Negro exploitation is the refusal of social recognition to individual Negroes of wealth or unusual ability. And this is why successful Negroes, no matter how rich and talented, have been unable to win a position of social equality with the American whites. Even where they have succeeded to a slight degree, their black fellows by the millions continue to carry the world on their bent backs.

24: REACHING FOR POWER

A RACE struggling for freedom and self-expression does not stop struggling merely because it is deserted by some of its ablest leaders or because it is thwarted or hampered by the vigilance and activity of the white, exploiting, ruling class. The American Negroes persisted in their efforts toward emancipation. The War of 1914-1918 gave them a crucial opportunity.

The war was fought ostensibly for democracy, freedom and self-determination. Negroes all over the world wanted these things. In Africa for fifty years they had felt the crushing weight of imperial exploitation. In the Americas since the days of slavery, they had performed the mass labor. When the war for democracy and peace was heralded by the white man's agencies of publicity, Negroes entered the armies and fought. From Africa they entered the armies of France. From the United States they entered the American armies in their segregated companies and segregated regiments.

Between June 5, 1917, and September 12, 1918, 2,290,527 Negroes registered for service in the United States Army. Negroes inducted into service numbered 367,710. With the regular army units and national guard units, the number of Negroes mobilized for the War was about 380,000. Of these Negro soldiers 200,000 went to France. (*Negro Year Book*, 1925-6, p. 250.)

Incidentally, while the American army was in France, efforts were made to prevent the French from "spoiling" the American Negro soldiers and officers. One widely spread circular called attention of the French to the subordinate position of the Negro in America and to the folly of giving them any encouragement in the direction of racial equality.

During the war crisis the American Negroes did something very much more important than entering the army. They migrated by hundreds of thousands from their field-hand jobs into centers of commerce and industry.

War demand for goods and the restrictions upon immigration created a labor market that opened a new field to Negro labor. "For the first time in American history opportunities, large in number, in skilled as well as unskilled labor, were offered to Negro workmen. They had served as the labor supply for the South, but the Northern field of labor had not been largely opened to them until the beginning of the World War. . . . In the period prior to the war, Negro labor had made its appearance for the first time in skilled industry." (Wesley, *Negro Labor in the United States*, p. 282.)

With the war-stimulated demand for labor went a corresponding increase in earning power. Wages rose. Negroes were not only able to secure positions as skilled workers, but they were able to command wages two, three, four or even five times those that they had earned as field hands or as artisans in the pre-war South. To be sure, prices also rose, but there was a real advance in purchasing power.

Higher income meant higher standards of living. Thus the war gave the American Negroes a chance to become "somebody" economically. They were no longer the dregs of the labor market, but an integral part of the American industrial labor supply. Negroes secured positions in some of the most important among the basic industries. By 1918 there were 4,000 Negroes employed by the Carnegie Steel Company in Pittsburgh. The Westinghouse Electric and Manufacturing Company had 1,500 Negroes in its employ. In 1916 the

Carnegie Steel Company had employed 1,500 Negroes and the Westinghouse Company 25. Under the jurisdiction of the United States Shipping Board 24,648 Negroes were employed. Among these one-fifth were engaged in skilled occupations. The United States Coal Commission reported 42,489 Negroes in the bituminous and anthracite mines. (Wesley, *Negro Labor in the United States*, pp. 295-6.) Before the war Negroes were a negligible factor in Detroit's industries. In 1922 there were over 500 Detroit plants employing Negroes. (*Ibid.*, p. 297.)

Following the war came the great labor struggles of 1919 to 1922. In the steel mills, in the mines, in the packing plants, on the railroads, among the dock workers, strikes took place in rapid succession. Again the Negroes came to the fore. Generally they had been excluded from trade unions or else they had been overlooked by trade union organizers. Now they became the chief strikebreaking force in the hands of the American ruling class.

Negro industrial experience in Chicago is summarized thus:

"Skilled positions were lost to colored men in the steel mills in the period of depression following the armistice, but were recovered during the steel strike of a year later. In the Stock Yards colored men also lost positions of skill, only to recover them during the strike of 1920-21 and gain others they never had. The great strike of 1919 and 1920 headed by John Kilkuski was lost by Polish workers, but resulted in promotions from unskilled to skilled positions in the plants of the International Harvester Company, Corn Products and Refining Company, and many other industries which are still held by colored men.

"Today the grey iron industry, insofar as molding is concerned, is practically all in the hands of colored men. Foundry after foundry has introduced the colored molder and when the white molder objects and leaves, the colored man gets control and keeps it. Colored foremen over men of their own race are not uncommon.

"The strike of the Stock Yards Union offered a chance for occupational advancement to colored men which was accepted. Carpenters', electricians' and steam-fitters' positions were given colored men, but were soon lost, in most instances, to returning strikers. . . .

"The recent strike of the railroad shop employees has, like all the others, brought advantages to the colored workman. Skilled positions formerly closed to him are now his. While no figures are available, it is known that many are working as boiler-makers, steam-fitters, carpenters and painters, in shops of Chicago.

"Similar advantages to the colored workman may be shown from every industrial dispute where colored persons are not members of the striking unions. There is no reason to conclude that the Negro is by choice a strikebreaker any more than other men, but the fact is that in most instances where he has risen above the ranks of a common laborer, the strike has furnished the medium through which his advancement is accomplished." (Wm. L. Evans, "The Negro in Chicago Industries," *Opportunity*, February, 1923, p. 15.)

Thus from 1915 to 1922 Negroes proved their worth in the industrial field. They proved to be good enough to take white men's jobs—jobs from which they had always been consistently excluded. If the Negro had been denied these jobs in competition with the white man before the war, during the war labor scarcity, and after the war in the labor conflicts when there were no white men left on the jobs, the Negro could take them, and he did.

Many Negroes were dismissed when the whites came back to work, but they have persisted in all the important industrial centers of the North. The war established the American Negro firmly as a factor in northern industry. It also proved, to the satisfaction of the white ruling class of the United States, that the Negro was an efficient strike breaker.

War and post-war experience showed three things clearly:

1. That the white ruling class of the United States, confronted by a labor shortage or a labor struggle with the white worker, would use the black worker.

2. That when the white ruling class was through with the black worker, it would replace him with a a white man if a white man proved more profitable or more desirable.

3. That the white ruling class was using the principle: "Divide and Rule" in its exploitation of American workers. It was splitting the workers along race lines and employing the blacks to crush the aspirations of the whites, then using the whites to drive the blacks into positions of inferiority.

The results of this war experience upon the American Negroes were far reaching and very significant:

1. The wealth of American Negroes increased rapidly. At the end of the Civil War the property in the hands of American Negroes was estimated at

$20,000,000. In 1923 Negro property was esti-
mated at $1,500,000,000. "Through purchase
and increase in value their property holdings are
increasing at the rate of about $50,000,000 a year.
The lands which they now own amount to more
than 22,000,000 acres or over 34,000 square miles,
an area greater than that of the five New England
states, New Hampshire, Vermont, Massachusetts,
Connecticut, Rhode Island. Home ownership is
an important phase of property accumulation. It
it estimated that Negroes now own over 600,000
homes; that is, one home out of every four which
they have established." (*Opportunity*, February,
1924, p. 42.)

The *Negro Year Book*, 1925-6 (page 1) prints the
following comparison of American Negro wealth:

	1866	1926
Homes Owned	12,000	700,000
Farms Operated	20,000	1,000,000
Businesses Conducted	2,100	70,000
Wealth Accumulated	$20,000,000	$2,000,000,000

2. Corresponding with this increase in Negro wealth
was a rising standard of Negro life. Negro
children were better cared for; diet was improved;
housing was more adequate.

Nowhere were the results of this advancing
standard more clearly indicated than in disease
rates and death rates. (Dublin, *Health and
Wealth*, pp. 261-264.) The death rate from
tuberculosis among Negro policy holders in the
Metropolitan Life Insurance Company declined 44
percent between 1911 and 1926. In 1911 the total
mortality rate for insured Negro children from 1
to 15 years of age was 10.1 per 1,000. In 1925 this

figure was reduced to 6.3 per 1,000 which is an improvement of 38 percent. (Pp. 263-4.) Dr. Dublin continues by pointing out that "the improvement in the sanitary conditions which surround the colored people is best evidenced by the decline in typhoid fever and pneumonia." He then cites evidence of the great advances they have been able to make in these directions.

3. Wider educational opportunities were included in the expanding economic standards of the American Negroes. Illiteracy decreased from 70 percent in 1880 to 22.9 percent in 1920. "Negro education in 1923 shows great progress when compared with that of former years. This is true with respect to equipment and facilities, both in public schools, secondary schools and in colleges." (*Opportunity*, February, 1924, pp. 42-3.)

4. Growing Negro communities in Southern as well as in Northern cities utilized the services of Negro lawyers, Negro doctors, Negro dentists and Negro real estate and insurance brokers. Negro merchants began to supply the needs of Negro customers. The Negro bourgeois class increased quickly in number, in wealth and in class consciousness and solidarity.

5. Negroes greatly increased the number and effectiveness of their racial organizations. And as Negro business and professional men were not admitted to the business and professional associations maintained by the whites, they established their own business and professional associations as a matter of course.

The bourgeois Negro built up an extensive Negro press (Detweiler, *The Negro Press*. See also enumeration of Negro newspapers, *Opportunity*, February,

1925, p. 51; December, 1925, p. 358; January, 1927, p. 7) and established Negro defense and relief societies. The National Association for the Advancement of Colored People specializes in legal defense work. The Urban League aims to advance the Negro economically.

At the same time Negro workers extended the organization of trade unions, and founded a Negro Labor Congress. A special survey (unpublished) of Negroes in trade unions, made by Charles S. Johnson for the Urban League during 1927-8 shows 65,492 Negro members (mostly in the North) in 48 national and international unions. In New York City Mr. Johnson found 14,500 Negroes in Unions; in Chicago, 13,000; in Detroit, 2,000. Mr. Johnson estimates Negro Union membership for the United States at 100,000.

Two generations of experience following the Civil War forced the Negroes into a position where they were compelled to organize for self defense and for self advancement and to act from a basis of race unity and race solidarity. The Negroes did not choose this position. They were forced as slaves to work for the ruling class in white America. After the Civil War and the legal termination of slavery, the continued race discrimination and race persecution made inevitable the development of a Negro race solidarity.

The war period with its expanding occupational opportunity, its advancing economic standards, and its multiplication of Negro organizations, was an era of enlarged Negro race consciousness. Negroes were members of an oppressed, exploited race. They were seeking for emancipation. "Democracy," "freedom," "self-determination" were ideas that grew quickly in the seed-ground of racial subjection. American Negroes decided to free themselves economically and socially—to emancipate themselves through their own efforts. They had become a race-conscious group, reaching for power.

25: BREAKING THE ECONOMIC SHACKLES

WITH the end of the war crisis and of the more intense forms of the labor conflict, the need for the Negro in industry grew less acute and the white ruling class began the process of returning him to his previous low economic level. This shift in standards was made more palatable by widespread talk of race cooperation.

Bourgeois Negro leaders who had believed that freedom and democracy would be won through the war, or would be given to the Negroes as a result of servility and obedience, protested against the pressure that was being put on the Negroes. They pointed to the war work done by Negroes. They emphasized Negro loyalty to the white man's government of the United States. They were met with the demand for racial cooperation.

Negroes were to be emancipated—but in accordance with a "pacific" formula. There was to be no more emphasis on race solidarity, no more talk of race conflict. Negroes were to gain their freedom without disturbing white domination.

T. J. Woofter, Jr., in his book on *Negro Migrations*, suggests that the Negro "extend the number of plants where he can work"; "extend the number of jobs within the plant which he can fill"; "increase his efficiency" and "develop his own organization and leadership which will cooperate with the constructive elements in the union." Negroes are to enter industry—but as inferiors.

"The most ambitious movement for better understanding between the races" in the opinion of W. D. Weatherford (*The Negro from Africa to America*, p. 450) "is the Inter-Racial Commission." "The Commission is composed of white and colored men and women including business men and professional men, college presidents and professors and representatives of the leading denominations." (*Idem.*) The Negro masses are to be emancipated through a commission appointed and dominated by whites, and on which labor is unrepresented.

Obviously these proposals have as their object the restoration of the Negro to his former position as a member of a subject, exploited race. "Readjustments" and "racial cooperation" in a country controlled exclusively by the whites means for the blacks the acceptance of whatever standards of race relationships the whites care to set up.

With the economic depression of 1927-1928 and the growing hard times came unemployment and wage cuts. The Negroes, generally unorganized and largely unskilled, were among the first to feel the economic pressure. The white ruling class was using the occasion to force the Negro masses back toward their former occupational levels and their former living standards. Depression in industry offered an occasion for returning the Negroes to their farm-hand jobs and keeping them economically in their places.

The Negroes have tasted the sweets of higher income, greater privileges, larger opportunities, broader life standards. They will not be so easily cajoled or coerced into accepting the lower standards which the ruling white class has decreed for them.

Nevertheless the whites continue the downward pressure. The blacks have but one alternative: to resist.

Events since the war have been numerous enough, and should have been plain enough to arouse or to intensify a widespread sense of race consciousness and a feeling of race solidarity among the American Negroes.

"When I was a little girl," said a Negro woman in her early thirties, "most colored people still lived in small streets. They just did not matter. Then came the war with high wages and new economic opportunities. Negroes could buy better things; own houses; move into better neighborhoods. Then they became dissatisfied." She cited the segregation law and the attempts through block agreements to restrict Negro living quarters.

In discussing the increase of race consciousness, E. B. Reuter (*The American Race Problem*, Chapter XVI, "Growth of Race Consciousness") calls attention to the effect of segregation in providing an opportunity and a vocation for Negro race leaders. The separation of the Negroes from the whites created a need for Negro professional and business men, and the growing sense of race solidarity made it possible for these business and professional men to prosper. Negro business men who could not have survived in free competition with the whites were patronized by the blacks because they were Negroes. The same thing is true of many Negro professional men and women. Negro slaves were not a separate group; they were knit into the fibre of society. But since the abolition of slavery the Negroes "at every point in their social evolution have met opposition and been reminded by persistent discrimination that they are a group apart." They have been denied full participation in the cultural life as well as in the economic life of the United States. Ambitious individuals striving to escape the inferior status have been forced back upon their own group. At every turn the Negroes have been made to realize that they will be tolerated only in the capacity of menials. (*Ibid.*, p. 398.)

Commenting on *The Voice of the Negro*, a collection of excerpts from Negro publications dealing with the post war position of the American Negro by Prof. R. T. Kerlin, W. D. Weatherford writes, "the total impression of the book is most alarming. It shows the horrible injustices which the Negro must suffer, and his attitude toward them. It shows a race no longer cringing and fawning, but a race at bay, long suffering, more than patient, but growing sullen and vindictive. It shows a people becoming conscious of its own power, proud of its own achievement and justly demanding fair treatment and respect." (*The Negro from Africa to America*, p. 473.)

Opportunity, for February, 1924 (p. 43), calls attention to the growing race consciousness of the Negro. "This growth is manifesting itself in various ways, important among· which are an increasing interest in race literature, more faith in race leadership, a demand for patronage of Negro business, a tendency to boycott white firms which do not treat the Negro with courtesy, and a tendency to move away from communities in which·lynchings have occurred."

The *Crisis*, particularly in its earlier years, was far more bitter. "When the American people in their carelessness and impudence have finally succeeded in welding ten million Negroes into one great self-guiding mass, they will realize their mistake. . . . In another generation, at the present rate, we will have in this country a mass of people of colored blood, acting together like one great fist for their own needs, with secret understanding, with pitiless efficiency, with resources for defense which will make their freedom incapable of attack from without. The actual organization of this group is progressing by leaps and bounds." (*Crisis*, December, 1913, p. 84.)

Less bitterly, E. B. Reuter writes, "In the present time a race-conscious Negro group is a largely accomplished fact. Its expression is, or is rapidly coming to be, as general as the activities and contracts of the race. There is, to be sure, a bitter internal strife among the factions striving for ascendancy, and the group is torn by endless class prejudices and personal jealousies, but back of the petty maneuvering of petty individuals, factions and classes is a fundamental trend of sentiment which may be discerned in widely separated fields and in otherwise unrelated activities." (*The American Race Problem*, p. 406.)

Experience is teaching the American Negro that an imperial ruling class such as that which now dominates public policy in the United States needs subject races to work and sometimes to fight. The imperialist rulers will take any necessary steps to hold the subject race in its subordinate position. If, in a crisis, they are compelled to grant the subject race privileges, they will take the first opportunity to withdraw them and to drive the members of the subject race back into their position as inferiors and menials.

The white ruling class of the United States is engaged in building a system of exploitation for profit and power. Even if it wished to do so, it could not free Negroes from this system. Emancipation must come from the exploited, not from the exploiters.

Recent Negro migrations into Northern cities—Chicago, Detroit, Cleveland, Buffalo, Pittsburgh, Philadelphia, New York—have brought masses of Negro workers into direct competition with white workers. The Negroes are at the bottom of the economic ladder—generally unskilled, almost wholly unorganized, members of a subject race, ideal victims for exploitation.

White employers are taking advantage of the Negroes—using them to force down wages, to break strikes.

White workers have not yet waked up to the situation. They still believe the ruling class propaganda about "racial inferiority." They still exclude Negroes from many of their working-class organizations.

Cheap Negro labor has been a source of profit to American exploiters for three hundred years. Today Negroes are organized to demand higher economic standards. White workers must back these demands to the limit.

Negro workers must join working-class organizations. They must help to build trade unions, cooperatives, a political party that represents working-class interests. Along no other path can the Negro masses hope for emancipation.

White workers must make every effort to bring the Negro workers into trade unions, into cooperatives, into a working-class political organization. There is no more vital task before the American workers today than that of establishing working-class solidarity across race lines.

There can be no victory for the working-class while workers are divided along race lines. Black and white workers must stand together for working-class emancipation.

Emancipation for the American Negro, as for any other subject race under the capitalist imperialist system, can come only when the Negro working masses have joined the white working masses in smashing the economic and social structure built upon individual and race exploitation, and by replacing it with a cooperative economic system under working-class control.

IMPORTANT FACTS

NEGRO POPULATION BY STATES
(in thousands)

State	1920	1960	State	1920	1960
Alabama	901	980	Nebraska	13	29
Arizona	8	43	Nevada	0.3	13
Arkansas	472	389	New Hampshire	0.6	2
California	39	884	New Jersey	117	515
Colorado	11	40	New Mexico	6	17
Connecticut	21	107	New York	198	1417
Delaware	30	61	North Carolina	763	1116
District of Columbia	110	412	North Dakota	0.5	0.7
Florida	329	880	Ohio	186	786
Georgia	1206	1122	Oklahoma	149	153
Idaho	0.9	1	Oregon	2	18
Illinois	182	1037	Pennsylvania	285	853
Indiana	81	269	Rhode Island	10	18
Iowa	19	25	South Carolina	865	829
Kansas	58	91	South Dakota	0.8	1
Kentucky	236	216	Tennessee	452	587
Louisiana	700	1039	Texas	742	1187
Maine	1	3	Utah	1	4
Maryland	244	518	Vermont	0.6	0.5
Massachusetts	45	112	Virginia	690	816
Michigan	60	717	Washington	7	49
Minnesota	9	22	West Virginia	86	89
Mississippi	935	916	Wisconsin	5	74
Missouri	178	391	Wyoming	1	2
Montana	2	1			

TOTAL AND NEGRO POPULATIONS OF THE UNITED STATES
(in millions) 1790 – 1960

Year	Total Population	Negro Population	Percent Negro
1960	179.3	18.9	9.9
1950	151.3	15.0	10.0
1940	131.7	12.9	9.3
1930	122.8	11.9	9.6
1920	105.7	10.5	9.9
1910	91.9	9.8	10.7
1900	75.9	8.8	11.6
1890	62.9	7.5	11.9
1880	50.1	6.6	13.1
1870	38.5	4.9	12.7
1860	31.4	4.4	14.1
1850	23.2	3.6	15.7
1840	17.1	2.9	16.8
1830	12.9	2.3	18.1
1820	9.6	1.8	18.4
1810	7.2	1.4	19.0
1800	5.3	1.0	18.9
1790	3.9	0.7	19.3

SLAVE POPULATION OF THE UNITED STATES
1790-1860

Year	United States	South	North	West
1860	3,953,760	3,838,765	114,966	29
1850	3,204,313	3,116,629	87,658	26
1840	2,487,355	2,427,986	59,369	—
1830	2,009,043	1,980,384	28,659	—
1820	1,538,022	1,508,692	29,330	—
1810	1,191,362	1,160,841	30,521	—
1800	893,602	857,097	36,505	—
1790	697,624	657,538	40,086	—

SLAVES AND SLAVE HOLDING FAMILIES
1790 AND 1850

Division and State	Number of Slave-Holding Families		Number of Slaves	
	1850	1870	1850	1870
United States	347,725	96,168	3,204,313	697,624
New England	———	2,147	———	3,763
Middle Atlantic ..	200	14,414	236	36,323
South Atlantic ..	169,264	77,242	1,663,397	641,691
East So. Central..	124,660	2,365	1,103,162	15,847
West So. Central..	34,416	———	350,070	———
West No. Central	19,185	———	87,422	———

APPROXIMATE PRICES OF SLAVES—1795-1860
(PRIME FIELD HANDS—MEN)

Year	Virginia	Georgia	New Orleans
1795	$200 - $300	——— - ———	——— - ———
1800	300 - 400	$400 - $500	$500 - $600
1805	400 - 500	500 - 600	600
1810	500	600	800
1815	400 - 500	500 - 600	600 - 700
1820	700	800	900 - 1,000
1825	400	700	800
1830	400 - 500	700 - 800	900 - 1,000
1835	600 - 700	1,000	1,100 - 1,200
1840	700 - 800	900 - 1,000	1,000 - 1,100
1845	500 - 600	600 - 700	700
1850	600 - 700	900 - 1,000	1,100
1855	1,000	1,300	1,300 - 1,400
1860	1,200 - 1,300	1,800	1,800

(Philips, *American Negro Slavery*, p. 370.)

NONWHITE POPULATION IN AMERICAN CITIES — 1960

City	Number of Non-whites (in thousands)	Percent of Total Population	City	Number of Non-whites (in thousands)	Percent of Total Population
Akron, O.	37.9	13.1	Greensboro, N.C.	31.1	26.0
Albany, N.Y.	10.9	8.5	Hammond, Ind.	2.6	2.3
Albuquerque, N.M.	5.9	2.9	Hartford, Conn.	25.1	15.5
Allentown, Pa.	0.8	0.8	Houston, Tex.	217.7	23.2
Amarillo, Tex.	8.0	5.8	Indianapolis, Ind.	98.7	20.7
Anaheim, Calif.	0.7	0.7	Jackson, Miss.	51.6	35.7
Atlanta, Ga.	186.8	38.3	Jacksonville, Fla.	82.7	41.2
Austin, Tex.	24.7	13.3	Jersey City, N.J.	37.3	13.5
Baltimore, Md.	328.4	35.0	Kansas City, Kan.	28.3	23.2
Baton Rouge, La.	46.6	29.9	Kansas City, Mo.	84.2	17.7
Beaumont, Tex.	35.0	29.4	Knoxville, Tenn.	20.9	18.7
Berkeley, Calif.	29.2	26.2	Lansing, Mich.	7.0	6.5
Birmingham, Ala.	135.3	39.7	Lincoln, Neb.	2.4	1.9
Boston, Mass.	68.4	9.8	Little Rock, Ark.	25.3	23.5
Bridgeport, Conn.	15.6	9.9	Long Beach, Calif.	14.8	4.3
Buffalo, N.Y.	73.4	13.8	Los Angeles, Calif.	417.2	16.8
Cambridge, Mass.	6.8	6.3	Louisville, Ky.	70.4	18.0
Camden, N.J.	27.9	23.8	Lubbock, Tex.	10.4	8.1
Canton, O.	11.1	9.8	Madison, Wis.	2.4	1.9
Charlotte, N.C.	56.5	28.0	Memphis, Tenn.	184.7	37.1
Chattanooga, Tenn.	43.2	33.2	Miami, Fla.	65.8	22.6
Chicago, Ill.	837.6	23.6	Milwaukee, Wis.	66.0	8.9
Cincinnati, O.	109.7	21.8	Minneapolis, Minn.	15.6	3.2
Cleveland, O.	253.1	28.9	Montgomery, Ala.	47.4	35.3
Columbus, Ga.	31.5	27.0	Nashville, Tenn.	64.8	37.9
Columbus, O.	78.3	16.6	New Bedford, Mass.	3.3	3.3
Corpus Christi, Tex.	9.3	5.6	New Haven, Conn.	22.7	14.9
Dallas, Tex.	131.2	19.3	New Orleans, La.	234.9	37.4
Dayton, O.	57.5	21.9	New York, N.Y.	1141.3	14.7
Dearborn, Mich.	0.1	0.1	Newark, N.J.	139.3	34.4
Denver, Colo.	35.3	7.1	Newport News, Va.	39.0	34.4
Des Moines, Iowa	10.5	5.1	Niagara Falls, N.Y.	7.7	7.5
Detroit, Mich.	487.2	29.2	Norfolk, Va.	80.6	26.4
Duluth, Minn.	1.1	1.1	Oakland, Calif.	97.0	26.4
Elizabeth, N.J.	11.9	11.0	Oklahoma City, Okla.	42.3	13.0
El Paso, Tex.	7.4	2.7	Omaha, Neb.	26.2	8.7
Erie, Pa.	6.7	4.9	Pasadena, Calif.	18.0	15.4
Evansville, Ind.	9.4	6.6	Paterson, N.J.	21.3	14.9
Flint, Mich.	34.8	17.7	Peoria, Ill.	10.0	9.5
Fort Wayne, Ind.	11.9	7.4	Philadelphia, Pa.	535.0	26.7
Fort Worth, Tex.	57.0	16.0	Phoenix, Ariz.	26.0	5.8
Fresno, Calif.	13.1	9.8	Pittsburgh, Pa.	101.7	16.8
Gary, Ind.	69.3	38.9	Portland, Ore.	20.9	5.6
Glendale, Calif.	0.6	0.5	Portsmouth, Va.	40.0	34.6
Grand Rapids, Mich.	14.8	8.3	Providence, R.I.	12.0	5.8

NONWHITE POPULATION IN AMERICAN CITIES — 1960 (*Cont.*)

City	Number of Non-whites (in thousands)	Percent of Total Population	City	Number of Non-whites (in thousands)	Percent of Total Population
Richmond, Va.	92.3	42.0	Springfield, Mass.	13.4	7.7
Rochester, N.Y.	24.2	7.6	Syracuse, N.Y.	12.3	5.7
Rockford, Ill.	5.4	4.3	Tacoma, Wash.	7.9	5.3
Sacramento, Calif.	25.0	12.7	Tampa, Fla.	46.4	16.9
St. Louis, Mo.	216.0	28.8	Toledo, O.	40.4	12.7
St. Paul, Minn.	9.3	3.0	Topeka, Kan.	9.8	8.2
St. Petersburg, Fla.	24.2	13.3	Torrance, Calif.	1.4	1.4
Salt Lake City, Utah	4.0	2.1	Trenton, N.J.	25.8	22.6
San Antonio, Tex.	43.2	7.4	Tucson, Ariz.	9.3	4.4
San Diego, Calif.	44.7	7.8	Tulsa, Okla.	26.0	10.0
San Francisco, Calif.	135.9	18.4	Utica, N.Y.	3.2	3.2
San Jose, Calif.	6.8	3.3	Washington, D.C.	418.7	54.8
Santa Ana, Calif.	2.7	2.7	Waterbury, Conn.	7.2	6.7
Savannah, Ga.	52.3	35.7	Wichita, Kan.	21.2	8.3
Scranton, Pa.	0.8	0.7	Wichita Falls, Tex.	8.5	8.4
Seattle, Wash.	46.5	8.4	Winston Salem, N.C.	41.2	37.1
Shreveport, La.	56.7	34.5	Worcester, Mass.	2.3	1.2
South Bend, Ind.	13.2	9.9	Yonkers, N.Y.	8.0	4.2
Spokane, Wash.	4.5	2.5	Youngstown, O.	31.9	19.1

URBAN AND RURAL WHITE AND NONWHITE POPULATIONS 1950 AND 1960 (percent distribution)

Area	1950			1960		
	Total	White	Nonwhite	Total	White	Nonwhite
Urban	64.0	64.3	61.7	69.9	69.5	72.4
Urbanized areas	45.8	45.8	45.3	53.5	52.7	58.9
Central cities	32.0	31.1	39.2	32.3	30.0	50.5
Urban fringe	13.8	14.7	6.1	21.1	22.8	8.4
Other urban	18.2	18.5	16.4	16.4	16.8	13.5
Rural	36.0	35.7	38.3	30.1	30.5	27.6

PROFESSIONAL, TECHNICAL, AND KINDRED WORKERS BY OCCUPATION

Occupation *	Total Male (in thousands)	Percent Nonwhite
All males	45,686	9.6
Professional, technical, and kindred workers	4,543	3.5
Accountants and auditors	396	1.4
Architects	30	2.3
Artists and art teachers	67	3.2
Authors, editors, and reporters	86	1.4
Chemists	77	3.4
Clergymen	197	7.7

IMPORTANT FACTS

PROFESSIONAL, TECHNICAL, AND KINDRED WORKERS BY OCCUPATION (*Cont.*)

Occupation *	Total Male (in thousands)	Percent Nonwhite
College presidents, professors, and instructors	140	4.0
Dentists	81	3.5
Designers and draftsmen	262	2.4
Engineers	552	1.7
Lawyers and judges	206	1.3
Musicians and music teachers	86	7.9
Natural scientists	59	2.8
Pharmacists	85	2.6
Physicians and surgeons	214	4.0
Social scientists	43	1.4
Social workers	58	11.1
Teachers, elementary	144	10.2
Teachers, secondary	276	5.8
Technicians, medical and dental	53	10.0
Technicians, electrical and electronic	89	3.0
Other professional and technical	971	3.5

* Some minor groups are omitted.

EMPLOYED PERSONS BY OCCUPATION AND COLOR — 1960 (Percentage Distribution)

Percent of total employed shown here by selected groups	White 59.6	Nonwhite 7.0
Occupational Group	Percent of Total Employed *	
White-collar workers		
Professional and technical workers	12.0	4.7
Managers, officials, and proprietors, except farm	11.6	2.5
Clerical workers	15.6	7.2
Sales workers	7.2	1.6
Blue-collar workers		
Craftsmen and foremen	13.7	5.9
Operatives	17.7	20.1
Laborers, except farm and mine	4.5	13.8
Service workers		
Private household workers	2.0	14.3
Other service workers	8.2	17.5
Farm workers		
Farmers and managers	4.3	3.1
Laborers and foremen	3.3	9.3

* Percentages have been rounded off.

NUMBER OF KINDERGARTENS FOR WHITES AND NEGROES IN SOUTHERN CITIES

City	White	Negro
Atlanta	40	0
Lexington	8	1
Louisville	42	7
Lynchburg	5	0
Memphis	0	0
New Orleans	46	0
Richmond	21	0
Winston-Salem	0	0

(Woofter, *Negro Problems in Cities*, p. 215.)

PER CAPITA SCHOOLS EXPENDITURES FOR WHITES AND NEGROES BY COUNTIES IN MISSISSIPPI

County	Total Population	Percent Negroes	Expenditure Per Capita Attendance White	Negro
Claiborne	13,019	78.2	$ 4.12	$1.00
DeSoto	24,359	76.0	14.34	2:00
Hinds	57,110	71.3	24.37	4.77
Issaquena	7,618	94.2	39.00	3.00
Yazoo	37,149	76.1	22.00	3.77
Jefferson	15,946	78.4	5.95	.84
Lowndes	27,632	71.0	3.90	.68
Madison	29,292	81.5	41.36	2.79
Marshall	26,105	72.2	12.00	3.15
Noxubia	23,710	84.0	60.32	4.80
Oktibbeha	16,872	64.4	25.50	3.82
Panola	27,845	67.9	22.93	3.24
Quitman	19,861	76.5	50.00	6.12
Sharkey	14,190	89.0	38.04	4.31
Sunflower	46,374	80.9	18.16	6.74
Tallahatchie	'35,953	69.4	30.55	3.50
Tunica	20,386	90.7	72.19	4.56
Washington	51,092	85.0	64.42	4.79
Wilkinson	15,319	76.9	25.08	4.27

(*Crisis*, December, 1926, p. 91)

LYNCHINGS IN THE UNITED STATES SINCE 1885

Year	White	Negro	Year	White	Negro
1885	106	78	1892	100	155
1886	67	71	1893	46	154
1887	42	80	1894	56	134
1888	47	95	1895	59	112
1889	81	95	1896	51	80
1890	37	90	1897	44	122
1891	71	121	1898	25	102

IMPORTANT FACTS

LYNCHINGS IN THE UNITED STATES SINCE 1885

Year	White	Negro	Year	White	Negro
1899	23	84	1914	3	49
1900	8	107	1915	13	54
1901	28	107	1916	4	50
1902	10	86	1917	2	36
1903	18	86	1918	4	60
1904	4	83	1919	7	76
1905	5	61	1920	8	53
1906	8	64	1921	5	59
1907	3	60	1922	6	51
1908	7	93	1923	4	29
1909	14	73	1924	0	16
1910	9	65	1925	0	17
1911	8	63	1926	7	23
1912	4	60	Total	1,045	3,205
1913	1	51			

Total of all lynchings........4,250

(*World Almanac*, 1928, p. 327)

LYNCHINGS BY STATES—1889-1924

State	White	Negro	State	White	Negro
Alabama	35	266	Nebraska	22	4
Arizona	13	1	Nevada	11	....
Arkansas	41	205	New Hampshire	....	....
California	30	5	New Jersey	....	....
Colorado	24	5	New Mexico	18	3
Connecticut	....	....	New York	1	1
Delaware	....	1	North Carolina	8	58
Dist. of Col.	....	....	North Dakota	10	1
Florida	14	218	Ohio	3	8
Georgia	24	433	Oklahoma	88	40
Idaho	12	1	Oregon	9	3
Illinois	12	13	Pennsylvania	....	3
Indiana	10	14	Rhode Island	....	....
Iowa	7	1	South Carolina	4	129
Kansas	13	12	South Dakota	18	....
Kentucky	46	123	Tennessee	36	162
Louisiana	50	287	Texas	54	283
Maine	....	....	Utah	....	1
Maryland	3	19	Vermont	....	....
Massachusetts	....	....	Virginia	8	75
Michigan	1	4	Washington	19	....
Minnesota	4	3	West Virginia	7	27
Mississippi	26	409	Wisconsin	4	....
Missouri	33	55	Wyoming	33	7
Montana	30	1			

(*World Almanac*, 1928, p. 327)

◆ 269 ◆

Number of Persons Lynched, by Offenses Charged and by Color—1889-1918

	Total	White	Percent of Total Whites Lynched	Negro	Percent of Total Negroes Lynched
Murder	1,219	319	45.4	900	35.7
Rape	523	46	6.6	477	19.0
Attacks upon Women	250	13	1.9	237	9.4
Other Crimes Against the Person	315	62	8.8	253	10.0
Crimes Against Property	331	121	17.2	210	8.3
Miscellaneous Crimes	438	135	19.2	303	12.0
Absence of Crime	148	6	.9	142	5.6
Total	3,224	702	100.0	2,522	100.0

(Thirty Years of Lynching, p. 36)

LIST OF BOOKS AND PUBLICATIONS CITED

American Labor Year Book, New York, Vanguard Press, 1927.

Blanshard, Paul, *Labor in Southern Cotton Mills*, New York, New Republic, 1927.

Bogart, E. L., *Economic History of the United States*, New York, Longmans, Green & Co., 1910.

Brown, W. H., *Educational and Economic Development of the Negro in Virginia*, University of Virginia Publications, No. 6.

Chicago Commission on Race Relations, *The Negro in Chicago*, Chicago, University of Chicago Press, 1922.

Children's Bureau, *Child Labor and the Work of Mothers on Gulf Truck Farms*, Washington, 1924.

Children's Bureau, *Child Labor on Maryland Truck Farms*, Washington, 1923.

Children's Bureau, *Welfare of Children in Cotton Growing Areas of Texas*, Washington, 1924.

Claridge, W. W., *History of the Gold Coast*, London, Murray, 1915. Vol. I.

Commission on Inter-Racial Cooperation, *Race Relations in 1927*, Atlanta, 1927.

The *Crisis*, Organ of the National Association for the Advancement of Colored People. Published monthly, New York.

Cutler, J. E., *Lynch Law*, New York, Longmans, Green & Co., 1905.

Detweiler, Frederick G., *The Negro Press in the United States*, Chicago, University of Chicago Press, 1922.

Dorsey, Hugh M., *As to the Negro in Georgia*, Atlanta, 1921. Reprinted by National Association for the Advancement of Colored People, New York, 1921.

Dowd, Jerome, *The Negro in American Life*, New York, Century, 1927.

Dublin, Louis I., *Health and Wealth*, New York, Harper Bros., Inc., 1928.

DuBois, W. E., *Suppression of the American Slave Trade*, New York, Longmans, Green & Co., 1896.

Duncan, H. G., *Changing Race Relationships in Border and Northern States*, Philadelphia, 1922.

Garner, James W., *Southern Politics Since the Civil War: Studies in Southern History and Politics*, New York, Columbia University Press, 1914.

Herskovits, Melville J., *The American Negro*, New York, Knopf, 1928.

Houghteling, Leila, *Income and Standards of Living of Unskilled Laborers in Chicago*, University of Chicago Press, 1927.

Kerlin, R. T., *Voice of the Negro*, New York, Dutton, 1920.

Locke, Alain, *The New Negro*, New York, Albert and Charles Boni, 1925.

Maryland Inter-Racial Commission Report, 1927.

Negro Year Book, Negro Year Book Publishing Co., Tuskegee Institute, Alabama, 1925-6.

Opportunity, a Journal of Negro Life, Published Monthly by the National Urban League, New York.

Ovington, M. W., *Half a Man*, New York, Longmans, Green & Co., 1911.

Paradise, Viola L., *Oyster and Shrimp Canning Communities on the Gulf Coast*, Children's Bureau, Washington, 1922.

Philadelphia Housing Association, *Negro Housing in Philadelphia*, Philadelphia, 1927.

Reuter, E. B., *The Mulatto in the United States*, Boston, Badger, 1918.

Reuter, E. B., *The American Race Problem*, New York, Crowell, 1927.

Spears, J. R., *American Slave Trade*, New York, Scribner's, 1901.

Street, Helen M., *Hospital and Dispensary Care of the Colored in Baltimore*, Johns Hopkins M. A. Thesis, June, 1927.

Thirty Years of Lynching in the United States, New York, National Association for the Advancement of Colored People, 1918.

Weatherford, W. D., *The Negro from Africa to America*, New York, Doran, 1924.

Wesley, C. H., *Negro Labor in the United States*, New York, Vanguard Press, 1927.

Woodson, C. G., *A Century of Negro Migration*, Washington, The Association for Study of Negro Life and History, 1918.

Woofter, T. J., Jr., *Negro Problems in Cities*, New York, Doubleday-Doran, 1928.

Woofter, T. J., Jr., *Negro Migration*, New York, Gray, 1920.

Work, Monroe N., *A Bibliography of the Negro in Africa and America*, New York, H. W. Wilson Co., 1928.

INDEX

Share cropping, 32
Skilled trades, exclusion of Negro from, 78, 154
Slave coast, 13
Slave trade, beginnings of, 14; profits of, 18
Slave population of U. S., 264
Slave revolts, 219
Slave-holding families, 264
Slaves, as artisans, 77; emancipation of, 220; geographic distribution of, 20, 21; runaways, 246; value of, 264
Slavery, conditions of, 16; outlawry of, 17; volume of, 17
Social position of Negro, 171 ff., 215; in North, 156, 157, 163 ff.; in South, 64, 169-70; in radical movement, 156, 157; of successful Negro, 247-48
South, see Black Belt
Sparrows Point, Md., Negro housing in, 112
Standards of living, Negro, in industrial centers, 120 ff., 126, 254; for Southern Negroes, 56 ff.; raised by War opportunity, 250 ff.
Strikes, post war, effect on Negroes, 251, 252
Strikebreakers, Negroes as, 252
Subject races, 5; Negro as, Chap. 20
Successful Negroes, 245-46
Sweet Case, 111

Theatres, exclusion of Negro from, 164
Trade schools for Negroes, 82
Trade union, exclusion of Negroes from, 84, 179; Negro, 256

Unemployment, 105, 106
Unskilled workers, 124, 154

Wages and income, of farm hands, 53, 54; of Negro children in South, 56; of Negro women in South, 56; of Negroes in industrial centers, 101, 102; of Southern Negroes, Chap. 7
Wage cuts for Negroes, 104
Washington, Negro housing in, 122
Wealth of Negroes, 254
White collar jobs for Negroes, 78-79
White domination, of economic life, 214, 258; in North, 127 ff.; of political life, 215, 217, 223 ff.; in South, 66, 68
White primary, 225
White race, superiority of, 155
Women workers, Negro, 124, 130
Working class organization, need of, 261
World War, effect on Negroes, 82, 249, 250, 252, 253, 254; number of Negroes in, 249

Y. M. C. A., Y. W. C. A., position of Negroes in, 177-78